UN: THE FIRST FIFTEEN YEARS

UN

THE FIRST FIFTEEN YEARS

CLARK M. EICHELBERGER

HARPER & BROTHERS · NEW YORK

CONTENTS

ACKNOWLEDGMENTS
ix

I   INTRODUCTION
1

II   PEACEFUL SETTLEMENT AND COLLECTIVE SECURITY
8

III   DISARMAMENT
36

IV   INDEPENDENCE, FREEDOM AND HUMAN RIGHTS
54

V   STANDARDS IN LARGER FREEDOM
76

VI   STRENGTHENING THE UNITED NATIONS
98

VII   ATTITUDE OF MEMBERS
124

To my colleagues—
James T. Shotwell, Benjamin V. Cohen,
Isaiah Bowman and Hamilton Fish Armstrong—
on the citizens committee
created by President Roosevelt to work with
Under Secretary of State Sumner Welles and
his associates in preparing the first American
working draft of what became the Charter of
the United Nations.

ACKNOWLEDGMENTS

The purpose of this book is to show that people and their governments must make a greater effort to give the United Nations the strength to prevent war and build peace in its broadest aspects. They cannot play at the United Nations, using it one day and ignoring it the next. It must be the very foundation of policy, not a diplomatic tool.

This volume attempts to present in a few bold strokes the development of the United Nations against the background of the human and scientific revolutions we have had to face. One shudders to think where the world might be today had it not been for the United Nations' meeting repeated crises in its first fifteen years.

Unless we are to end it all with a nuclear explosion, the scientific and human revolution will continue. Inevitably then, the United Nations must grow accordingly.

If I were to thank all of the people who have helped me, I would have to go back to the early days of the League of Nations and mention many people who have helped me formulate my opinions about the development of international society.

If I seem to have given too much attention to the role of the United States in the United Nations, I am sure my colleagues abroad will understand that I have written this book particularly for the American public.

I am indebted to many people who have helped me with portions of this volume, but I want to mention particularly

Professor Arthur N. Holcombe and Professor John G. Stoessinger, who read the manuscript in its entirety. I wish especially to thank my colleague Margaret Olson, who again contributed so very much in ideas and fact.

M. E.

UN: THE FIRST FIFTEEN YEARS

I

INTRODUCTION

The United Nations is fifteen years old. These years have seen scientific, economic and political changes which stamp them as one of the great revolutionary periods of history. The United Nations has been the deciding factor in helping the world survive these changes. And in so doing, it has been profoundly changed. The interpretation of the Charter and the machinery itself are vastly different than contemplated at San Francisco, when the Charter was drafted.

The Scientific Revolution

The first decade after the war witnessed the beginning of the atomic age. The second decade may be identified with the beginning of interplanetary travel. As one looks back at the San Francisco Conference, he senses that the statesmen who were drafting the Charter were unaware that atomic bombs would soon be dropped, ending the war quickly; and that these atomic bombs would profoundly change the security calculations upon which the Charter was based.

Scarcely had the nations accepted the possibility of atomic destruction or the use of atoms for peace, when another horizon was penetrated—the horizon of outer space. The latter presents the world with greater possibilities of adventure and more profound moral decisions than atomic energy.

What steps have been taken in the United Nations to meet the challenge of the scientific revolution and what steps are contemplated will appear in succeeding chapters.

The Revolt of Colonial Peoples

Seven hundred million people, over one-fourth of the world's population, have thrown off the yoke of colonialism since the Second World War ended. Freedom is coming to Africa, the last extensive bastion of colonialism, at a rate no one could have imagined five years ago. Indeed, before the second decade of the United Nations ends, only a very few of the most scattered or primitive peoples will be without self-government. The Trusteeship Council may disappear.

The rapidity of this development was not anticipated at San Francisco, although its seeds were planted in the Organization. The Charter of the United Nations has become a charter of liberty through which colonial peoples can appeal for freedom. The Organization itself, particularly the General Assembly and the Trusteeship Council, has provided the forum in which appeals for freedom can be made.

For some time, the Soviet veto primarily, together with an American-influenced majority in the Security Council, prevented many states from entering the United Nations. The log-jam was broken in 1955. Now one-fourth of the membership of the United Nations is made up of new states. These new states have made a profound change in the power balance of the Organization.

The Revolt Against Misery

Accompanying the revolt against colonialism is the revolt against hunger. The half of the world that is miserable is deciding that it is not necessary for it to be so always.

The problem is overwhelming. Some of the peoples to be aided have rich and ancient cultures but are up a blind alley economically. Others are so primitive that they have not discovered the use of the wheel. And the increasing efficiency of Western technology is actually increasing the disparity between the "haves" and the "have-nots."

An unparalleled effort is being made on the part of the nations, multilaterally through the United Nations and individually, to meet the problems of the underprivileged peoples.

The challenge is to help a considerable part of the world leap from the Middle Ages to the twentieth century in a few years. Assuming the danger of war is put far in the background, disarmament achieved and the colonial peoples freed, the problem of the underprivileged will remain the most absorbing problem.

Breakup of the Five-Power System

Another change which the United Nations has had to survive, to adjust itself to, and if possible to turn to good account, has been the breakup of the five-power system and the creeping paralysis of the cold war.

The late Secretary of State Stettinius, in presenting the United Nations Charter to the Senate Foreign Relations Committee in 1945, explained that giving the great powers permanent seats and the veto in the Security Council was simply recognizing the power facts of life. The United Nations, he said, would depend for its success upon the unanimity of the five great powers. Others referred to the five as the world policemen, who would keep order for years to come.

Where is the five-power system now? The cold war quickly separated the Soviet Union from the other four. The government of Nationalist China went into exile on Formosa.

One might say that the final breakup of the five-power system in the United Nations occurred in 1956 when the United Kingdom and France vetoed a resolution in the Security Council over Suez, and the Soviet Union vetoed a resolution urging it to desist from armed intervention in Hungary. These vetoes led to two extraordinary and simultaneous sessions of the General Assembly in which the United States was the only great power willing to assume its Security Council obligations under the Charter in all circumstances.

Even had there been no cold war, it was a mistake in 1945 to assume that all five great powers would remain united. It was a mistake to assume that the other members would be content with the domination of five. Indeed, the Charter could not in 1945 determine which nations would be the five great powers in the indefinite future.

UN: The Decisive Factor for Peace

The last fifteen years have been years of unparalleled change, danger and bold adventure. Scientific horizons have been penetrated. A great part of the world has won its independence. An effort is being made to share the productive capacities of the more fortunate with the underprivileged.

At the same time, many efforts at improvement were chilled by the paralyzing effect of Communism, which, at least for the first ten years after the war, continued to expand. The problem was made even more difficult by the fact that the Soviet Union made the first imaginative foray into outer space.

What has kept the peace in these fantastic fifteen years? The Marshall Plan? It saved the West from bankruptcy. NATO? It may well have saved Western Europe from invasion. The Organization of American States? Certainly it continued the protective mantle of the Monroe Doctrine around the nations of the southern part of the Western Hemisphere. The Baghdad Pact and the Eisenhower Doctrine? Their beneficial effects are questionable. The nuclear stalemate? Here is the peace of fear, for each side in the bipolarized world knows that an initiative on its part would be met by instant retaliation, so that all would be destroyed.

However, the decisive factor for world peace has been the United Nations. It has made the difference between the uneasy peace in which the world has lived and a Third World War. Every day since the Second World War there has been spasmodic fighting somewhere on earth, but these conflicts have not resulted in a Third World War. The United Nations has made the difference. It is hard to define the many specific and subtle influences of the United Nations on the side of peace. One phrase, however, may best describe it—"moral unity."

Suppose the nations had entered the atomic age in a world of anarchy. The author knows from interviews with the late President Roosevelt that he feared a repetition of the reaction of 1920 which kept the United States out of the League of Nations. He was determined that at least a provisional United Nations be created before the fighting ended.

What if the United Nations allies had not carried out President Roosevelt's intention? What if the nations had not formally adopted principles of good conduct with laws against war? Suppose they had not created a common meeting place, with machinery for the peaceful settlement of disputes? Suppose they had not provided a forum in which the peoples dominated by colonialism could petition peacefully for their freedom? Suppose the newly created United Nations and specialized agencies had not set in motion a process for the relief of economic misery? If these things had not been done it is doubtful that the world would have survived this long. The changes in the postwar period were so great and so terrible in their potential for destruction that without the unifying force of the United Nations the world might well have destroyed itself.

On the eve of the Fifteenth Assembly, eighty-two states are legally bound by the obligations of the Charter. The peace of the world is dependent upon their becoming increasingly integrated into an international society by the many bonds which the United Nations provides. It is essential that this moral unity be strengthened every day by devotion and common usage. The ever-present danger is that this sense of moral unity be weakened; that the nations fragmentize their concerns by alliances and bilateral action.

So far the United Nations has survived one attack after another, one neglect after another, and has emerged stronger than ever. Nations may ignore it for a moment, but they finally return to it as the best means to meet their problems.

Now a new form of danger appears. In its fourteenth and fifteenth years the United Nations has been by-passed by the great powers, including the United States, more consistently than during its early years. It may be that some of the great powers are more prosperous and feel less need of the fraternity of mankind than they did during the Second World War and its immediate aftermath. Some of the great powers may be fearful of their roles in the United Nations because of the addition of so many new states. They can no longer control the United Nations through the power of the veto in the Security Council. They cannot be sure of a majority in the General Assembly.

A danger developed that some of the powers might attempt to create a directorate of the great powers through a series of summit conferences outside the United Nations. The great powers might attempt to create disarmament machinery with only a passing reference to the world organization. Such steps could mean a serious weakening of the efforts to establish an international society on which peace would finally depend.

The summit conference of May 16, 1960, broke up before it could consider the problems that brought it together. The cold war has been intensified rather than lessened as was anticipated. Bitterness and recrimination between East and West may be the fashion for some months to come. In this situation, it is very important that the United Nations be used to maintain the moral solidarity of the world society. It must function as an avenue by which East and West can be brought together by public and private diplomacy. It must be the means through which many nations can put moral pressure upon the nuclear giants again to relax tensions and use its machinery to settle their difficulties.

II

PEACEFUL SETTLEMENT
AND COLLECTIVE SECURITY

The purpose of the United Nations is to prevent war.

The United Nations was born in the tragedy of the Second World War. When the framers of the Charter met in San Francisco, Allied forces were fighting beyond the German frontier and the forces in the Pacific were island-hopping before the assault on Japan could begin. The Charter begins by stating that the peoples of the world are combining their efforts to accomplish certain objectives:

Understandably, the first objective was ". . . to save succeeding generations from the scourge of war, which twice in our lifetime has brought untold sorrow to mankind. . . ."

Because they were aware that conflict began with the violation of human rights in Germany and Italy, the framers declared as the next objective ". . . to reaffirm faith in fundamental human rights, in the dignity and worth of the human person, in the equal rights of men and women and of nations large and small. . . ."

In the third paragraph the framers returned to the political side and determined ". . . to establish conditions under which justice and respect for the obligations arising from treaties and other sources of international law can be maintained. . . ."

And finally, looking forward to the prospect of a better life when the scourge of war was removed, they wrote as a fourth objective ". . . to promote social progress and better standards of life in larger freedom."

There is a fine logic in the sequence of these four objectives. The first and third are based on the prevention of war and the establishment of peaceful processes. The second and fourth reaffirm faith in human rights and social progress. They look toward the removal of the basic causes of war and anticipate a better way of life in which war would be thought of less and less.

The total purpose then of the United Nations is the maintenance of peace. The over-all method by which it is to be accomplished is the development of a dynamic international society in which nations are held together by many visible and intangible bonds of civilized adjustment and development. As man develops the means of total destruction and the capacity to explore celestial bodies, the scope of the dynamic international society must continue to grow. One dreams of an order in which nations will be so enmeshed in co-operative peaceful efforts that serious political disputes and threats of war will be relegated to minor roles.

A peaceful and just society requires civilized methods of adjustment. The United Nations increasingly provides them. These methods may be of various kinds, including debates in the General Assembly or informal conferences in the Delegates' Lounge at headquarters. Various technical conferences include scientists, doctors, businessmen, labor leaders, university professors and farmers. Constant contacts in many areas of human living set the climate and method of adjustment and provide an atmosphere of permanence. Hundreds of regular and *ad hoc* meetings take place annually. There are times when the problems of adjustment become sharper. Then one enters the realm of disputes which must be settled, or imminent or actual aggression which must be prevented or stopped.

This chapter will deal with the work of the United Nations in (a) settling disputes that might lead to conflict, and (b) preventing or stopping aggression.

Chapter VI of the Charter is entitled "Pacific Settlement of Disputes." Chapter VII of the Charter is entitled "Action with Respect to Threats to the Peace, Breaches of the Peace, and Acts of Aggression."

The Charter suggests a variety of means for dealing with disputes. It prefers that the nations first resort to normal diplomacy. The parties to any dispute ". . . the continuance of which is likely to endanger the maintenance of international peace and security, shall, first of all, seek a solution by negotiation, enquiry, mediation, conciliation, arbitration, judicial settlement, resort to regional agencies or arrangements, or other peaceful means of their own choice." But back of this wide variety is presumed to be the firm hand of the Security Council, ready to act under Chapter VI, and the moral authority of the General Assembly. The hand of the Security Council becomes firmer as that body moves from Chapter VI to Chapter VII, which gives it authority to act to prevent or stop aggression.

The members of the United Nations confer upon the Security Council the ". . . primary responsibility for the maintenance of international peace and security, and agree that in carrying out its duties under this responsibility the Security Council acts on their behalf."

The authority of the General Assembly as defined in the Charter is broad, but less precise as far as the maintenance of peace and security are concerned. That body ". . . may discuss any questions or any matters within the scope of the present Charter or relating to the powers and functions of any organs provided for in the present Charter. . . ." It ". . . may consider the general principles of co-operation in the maintenance of international peace and security. . . ." It ". . . may discuss any questions relating to the maintenance of international peace and security brought before it by any Member of the United Nations, or by the Security Council, or by a state which is not a Member of the United Nations. . . ."

Fifteen years have passed since the above clauses were adopted. United Nations practice demonstrates a considerable departure from the role of the Security Council and the General Assembly as written in the Charter. In the process of peacemaking the United Nations has developed methods and techniques which could scarcely have been contemplated at the San Francisco Conference.

The outreach of the United Nations in preventing war is very great indeed. Military men borrowed from various countries are guarding mountain passes in Kashmir to prevent conflict between Pakistani and Indian armies. A United Nations "peace" force called UNEF is guarding the border between Israel and Egypt in the Gaza Strip and the Sinai Peninsula. A unit of UNEF is also stationed in the Sharm el Sheikh area at the Gulf of Aqaba. A United Nations "presence" is a factor in guaranteeing the independence and stability of Jordan. An equivalent of a United Nations "presence" is representing the United Nations in Laos. A considerable United Nations army is guarding the armistice line at the Thirty-eighth Parallel in Korea.

As we shall presently see, the Security Council has declined in authority. The General Assembly has assumed precise peacemaking functions. The role of the Secretary-General in this field has been greatly enhanced.

Shifting Responsibilities

The idea of a small Security Council in constant session developed during the war. In the days preceding the San Francisco Conference, statesmen were heard to speak of the big policemen. They were the big powers who, having made the major total contribution, if not the largest relative contribution, to victory, were going to police the world. It was thought that the United States, the United Kingdom and the Soviet Union on a world scale, China as far as the Pacific area was concerned and France, possibly to be admitted to the club later, would be the policemen who would keep the peace at least through the reconstruction period.

The success of the United Nations has not depended on the unanimity of the great powers. In consequence the United Nations has lived and grown in unexpected ways.

An examination of the meetings which the Security Council has held year by year indicates a general decline, despite the fact that the Security Council is set up technically to be in continuous session. Its rules of procedure call for a meeting every two weeks. Nevertheless, the record of Security Council meetings is as follows: 1946—88; 1947—137; 1948—168; 1949—62; 1950—73; 1951—39; 1952—42; 1953—42; 1954—32; 1955—23; 1956—50; 1957—49; 1958—36; 1959—5. The trend may be reversing itself. It is anticipated that there will be at least thirty Security Council meetings in 1960—possibly many more.

It should be pointed out that the members of the Security Council are consulted privately and informally by the Secretary-General in steps to strengthen peace. Consequently the Council has more influence than its present number of meetings would indicate.

In comparison, a list of the number of days each year that the General Assembly has been in session will show, in addition to regular sessions, three emergency sessions and two special sessions. The General Assembly twice has remained in active or suspended session until the next Assembly met.

The Secretary-General has tended to be more and more on the road on peacemaking business. In some of his travels he has been engaged in the adjustment or peaceful settlement of disputes at the request of the General Assembly or the Security Council or on his own initiative. Other of his travels have been visits to new areas or to attend meetings of various United Nations commissions, committees or scientific conferences.

What happened to reduce the number of Security Council meetings from a high of 168 in 1948 to a low of 5 in 1959? Certainly the number of disputes has not lessened proportionately. International tensions have increased. But the Security Council has gradually relinquished its functions as the body primarily responsible for the maintenance of international peace and security. The General Assembly has assumed, and the Secretary-General has been asked to assume, more and more of the peacemaking functions of the Organization. However, it should be pointed out that the General Assembly in various resolutions has scrupulously recognized the primary responsibility of the Security Council in the maintenance of peace and security.

What have been the reasons for this shift in authority? The reasons for the decline of the Security Council as far as this chapter is concerned could be said to be: the expansion of the cold war, the abuse of the veto, lack of adequate geographical distribution of its seats and, since 1950, the absence of delegates representing the people on the mainland of China. In the first fifteen years of the United Nations, the Soviet Union cast eighty-seven vetoes. Forty-nine were cast against the admission of new states. The rest were pri-

marily against efforts of the Security Council to move toward
the settlement of disputes.

Closely allied with the veto is the spread of the cold war.
Whenever its chilling effect was absent, the Security Council
could function as was intended. But as the cold war extended to one geographical area after another the Security
Council was proportionately reduced in influence. The cold
war finally reached the Middle East. In the early days, the
Soviet Union supported the establishment of the state of
Israel. Today, a Soviet veto against Israel would be anticipated in any dispute between Israel and her Arab neighbors
before the Security Council.

The Chinese seat in the Security Council is now held by
the Nationalist government in exile on Formosa. Six hundred
fifty million people on the mainland, controlled by an aggressive government, are not represented. It is difficult
to bring problems of the Far East to the United Nations
in the absence of that government. Indeed, it is difficult
to hold summit conferences in the Security Council for
the same reason.

The Charter provides that the members of the Security
Council shall be selected with due regard paid ". . . in the
first instance to the contribution of Members of the United
Nations to the maintenance of international peace and
security and to the other purposes of the Organization, and
also to equitable geographical distribution." These criteria
have frequently been overlooked. Certain areas, such as
Asia, have never been adequately represented on the Security
Council.

While the United States criticizes the Soviet Union for
repeated abuse of the veto, the Soviet Union on the other
hand refers to the built-in majority of the United States
on the Security Council. It points to the fact that there have

been as many as nine military allies of the United States
on the Council at the same time.

Even if the cold war and the veto had not reduced the
capacity of the Security Council to function, the Assembly
would have become the paramount body as the years went
on because it is the most representative body of the Organization. As many new nations joined the United Nations,
their chance of being represented on the Security Council
became less. They have sought expression in the General
Assembly.

Achievements of the Security Council

The Security Council has many achievements to its credit.
Its first act was the mobilization of public opinion to force
withdrawal of Soviet troops from Iran in 1946. The last act
of its fourteenth year was sending a group to Laos to secure
information about border infiltrations from North Vietnam.

The Security Council has a record of important decisions
that have prevented war. Any critical meeting is widely
attended by the public and widely reported. Representatives
of many countries watch the deliberations, hoping with all
their hearts that the eleven men around the horseshoe table
will be able to make decisions and enforce them. The public
feels that these eleven men with proper authority from their
governments and with courage in their hearts can make
important decisions. And these decisions can be backed by
a strength of action authorized by provisions of the Charter.

The strongest provisions for supranational authority are
to be found in Articles 24, 25 and 26. Here the members
confer on the Security Council primary responsibility for
the maintenance of international peace and security and
they ". . . agree to accept and carry out the decisions of
the Security Council in accordance with the present Char-

ter." That is, unequivocally all but the big five with the veto. But even these five took a pledge at San Francisco that the use of the veto would be sparing and prudent.

Ironically, the Security Council took its strongest action against aggression when in June, 1950 it passed two resolutions authorizing resistance to aggression in Korea. For a brief moment, the Soviet Union was boycotting the Security Council as a demonstration against the absence of a Chinese Communist delegate in place of the Nationalist government delegate. Consequently, the Security Council could act quickly, without the Soviet veto. Sensing its mistake, the Soviet Union sent back its representative. While he could not undo the unanimous vote, which authorized and ordered resistance to aggression at the Thirty-eighth Parallel, he could by a veto prevent the Security Council from implementing its decisions.

Consequently, when the General Assembly met for its fifth session, it adopted the Uniting for Peace Resolution. This historic resolution gave unanticipated concrete meaning to the general provisions of the Charter. As has happened in other historic events, a constitution was given a precise meaning to enable it to meet a crisis and survive.

The Uniting for Peace Resolution provides that should the Security Council be prevented from performing its duties in the maintenance of peace and security because of a veto, the General Assembly can take over. No revision of the Charter is necessary. A simple revision of the Rules of Procedure provided that the General Assembly can be called into session within twenty-four hours instead of fifteen days, by a simple vote of seven of the Security Council or a majority of the members of the United Nations.

The value of the Uniting for Peace Resolution was doubly demonstrated in 1956. Israeli troops, goaded by great provocation from Egypt, were racing across the Sinai Peninsula.

The United States asked for an emergency meeting of the Security Council. It introduced a resolution calling upon Israel to withdraw these troops. The British and the French delegates cast vetoes against the American resolution. They announced they had given an ultimatum to Egypt to permit landing of their troops in Suez. Immediately, the United States joined in a request for an emergency meeting of the General Assembly. The simple majority of seven members of the Security Council agreed. And the General Assembly met in an extraordinary session the next day.

A few days later, about three o'clock in the morning, the General Assembly, which was in an all-night session considering the problem of Suez, recessed for another emergency meeting of the Security Council to hear a complaint that Soviet troops were invading Hungary. Again there was an American resolution to desist. Again there was a veto, this time by the Soviet Union. Again there was a move on the part of the United States for an emergency meeting of the General Assembly. The Assembly met in another emergency session the next day. Thus there were two emergency sessions of the General Assembly going on simultaneously.

New Methods to Deal with New Problems

A separate volume would be necessary if one were to describe the number of disputes before the United Nations and the various methods used to deal with them. Secretary-General Trygve Lie, in his report to the Fourth General Assembly, said: "United Nations action in other parts of the world has also contributed to the progress made towards a more peaceful world by either preventing or ending wars involving five hundred million people."

The United Nations has acted with much flexibility, imagination and courage in dealing with disputes. It has developed methods and techniques which, although not spelled

out in the Charter, have their authority in articles out-
lining the competence of the Security Council and the
General Assembly.

The Security Council or the General Assembly has appointed commissions to watch troubled frontiers such as
the Greek border and the Thirty-eighth Parallel in Korea.
Both steps resulted from a liberal interpretation of the
right of both bodies to establish such subsidiary organs
as they deem necessary for the performance of their functions. Also the General Assembly can initiate studies and
the Security Council may investigate any troublesome dispute or situation. Successful actions by the Security Council
and the General Assembly combined in 1958 to avoid war
in the Middle East.

Sometimes the Security Council and the General Assembly have furnished safety valves to air grievances and to
bring the force of world public opinion on problems and
injustices which seem insoluble. The Security Council on
March 30, 1960, began a series of meetings to hear the
complaint of twenty-nine members against the treatment
of nonwhites by the South African government.

The value for the world of having a place of protest is
almost incalculable. It relieves pressures that might otherwise find their expression in bloodshed and revolt.

In some cases the United Nations has been able to stop
the fighting and secure an armistice but has not been able
to translate the armistice into peaceful settlements. The reasons are obvious. Some of the causes of conflict go back
to antiquity. In other cases the immediate parties to a dispute, and most of the members of the United Nations, will
take action to stop or prevent fighting which might produce
a world catastrophe but are not willing to make the additional sacrifice of immediate national interests for permanent peace settlements.

The United Nations stopped aggression in Korea and forced the aggressor behind the Thirty-eighth Parallel with considerable loss of life. It secured an armistice. It has not yet been able to achieve an agreement on the Korean problem and the unification of that unhappy peninsula.

The United Nations stopped the fighting between India and Pakistan. Its truce teams are still guarding the lines between the opposing forces, but it has not yet been able to hold the plebiscite to which both sides agreed.

The United Nations secured armistice agreements between Israel and the Arab states. Mixed commissions supervise the armistice lines and the United Nations Emergency Force protects one of them. But the Organization has not been able to translate the armistice agreements into final peace settlements.

In fifteen years the United Nations has not been able to uproot the historic causes of war, but it has been able to prevent general war. Sporadic fighting has gone on almost every day, but the United Nations has checked it before world conflict developed.

This, however, is not the whole story. The United Nations has some definite peace settlements to its credit. It has tackled the historic causes of war on a broad front. Racial antagonism, economic misery and political tension are being faced through many efforts. These efforts range from the educational program of UNESCO to the debates on political tensions in the General Assembly.

Collective Security

The United Nations should be able to prevent or stop aggression in any case where one of the parties will not accept peaceful settlement. This would be the ideal state of international society. The Charter of the United Nations so recognizes these two functions by describing Chapter VI as the "Pacific Settlement of Disputes" and Chapter VII as "Action with Respect to Threats to the Peace, Breaches of the Peace, and Acts of Aggression." In practice, however, there has not always been a clear-cut distinction between the two functions. It would be difficult to place some of the acts of the United Nations to maintain peace as falling exclusively under one category.

From the establishment of the League of Nations to date, the possibility of organized resistance to aggression has been called collective security. Collective security involves certain legal procedures previously agreed to. There must be a legally constituted international body capable of passing judgment on the facts of aggression based upon previously accepted law. Following the determination of such facts, a legally constituted body must authorize resistance to aggression. Machinery for collective action must be accompanied by an accepted obligation of the members of the world society to resist aggression regionally or universally if called upon. And finally, it is assumed that there must be a collective force, potential or in being, which can be used to stop aggression. The force can be diplomatic, military or economic. These elements for collective security are to be found in the United Nations Charter.

Collective Action in Korea

United Nations resistance to aggression at the Thirty-eighth Parallel in Korea, undertaken on the initiative of the United States, was history's most nearly complete example of collective security. The facts of aggression were certified to by an agency of the United Nations. This certification was so complete that when the Security Council met on June 25, 1950 to consider the aggression no nation dared ask for a delay on the excuse that the facts were not known.

This was a far cry from 1932 when the League of Nations dispatched the Lytton Commission to secure the facts in Manchuria. By the time the Commission had traveled to the Pacific area, by train and by boat, and formulated its condemnation of Japan, the Japanese had taken Manchuria.

In the case of Korea, the Security Council acted quickly. Resistance to aggression was authorized, step by step, by the legally constituted bodies of the United Nations. The basic resolutions placing the United Nations against aggression were passed by the Security Council in the absence of the Soviet Union. Later, when Soviet tactics made it impossible for the Security Council further to implement its resolutions authorizing resistance to aggression, the General Assembly took over the direction of events.

The burden of resistance to aggression was shared at least in some degree by a large number of United Nations members. Sixteen nations sent fighting forces. Two members sent heroic hospital units. Additional contingents could have been supplied had the logistics been arranged. Almost forty nations sent material aid of some kind. And finally, there was a United Nations command. The Security Council asked the President of the United States to name a supreme commander under whose authority the national contingents would fight.

It is true that there have been other examples of collective action, when nations co-operated under a supreme commander to resist aggression. Such was the case of Allied resistance to German aggression in the First and Second World Wars. However, such resistance was never authorized by the established body of the world community. Indeed, had the League of Nations authorized resistance to aggression the day the German army attacked Poland, the League might well have been the moral force guiding the nations during the Second World War. It might then have gained new stature and made the establishment of the United Nations to take its place unnecessary.

Korea gave the world hope that the nations could take collective action, if not against a great power, certainly against the satellite of a great power.

There was boldness in 1950. President Truman took a historic decision. With breath-taking speed, the United Nations responded to United States initiative. The results were felt in many directions. What might have been a chain of aggressions was interrupted and a Third World War averted. Western Europe particularly took heart because aggression could be met and stopped. The Atlantic Community took on additional vitality and the NATO forces developed. It has been said the United Nations was prevented from going the way of the League of Nations by its action in Korea.

It seems important to devote some attention to the way collective security operated in Korea because it gives us lessons for the future.

Certain weaknesses were revealed both in the co-operation of member states and in the machinery and procedures of collective security. There was an unevenness in the determination of the governments to fulfill their obligations. The nations had not complied with Article 43 of the Charter to designate forces for use by the Security Council. Consequently, the United States, because it had military forces nearby, was called upon to make a disproportionate contribution of men and matériel. The acceptance of contingents and building them into a truly international army was a matter of improvisation.

The United Nations lacked a general staff that might have appointed a supreme commander and assessed the political consequences of his acts in the field. The Military

Staff Committee provided by the Charter was unworkable. The Soviet Union was a member of it and was allied with Communist China. The Military Staff Committee did not bear adequate relationship to the nations that had fighting forces in Korea. As an alternative, these nations developed an *ad hoc* basis for co-ordination of military efforts. The diplomatic representatives met regularly at the Department of State in Washington. Consequently, collective action was more and more directed by Washington instead of by the United Nations. And some of the nations were altogether too willing to leave the military operations with accompanying praise and blame to the United States. And American military men were quite willing to accept this responsibility.

In retrospect, it appears that the United Nations should have been attempting negotiations for peaceful settlement while resistance was going on. In fact, confidential diplomatic talks had been going on to secure a neutral zone along the Yalu River, but military events rendered them futile. Somewhere in this evolving situation the decision was made to march to the Yalu River. This decision was a tragic mistake. It resulted in military disaster.

On October 7, the General Assembly passed an ambiguously worded resolution that the United Nations High Command could interpret as giving it authority to occupy all of North Korea in order to unify the country. One delegate in the Assembly Hall warned against this northward march. The Indian delegate told the Assembly that his government had information that, if such a course were pursued, the area of conflict might be extended.

On October 21, 1950, the Supreme Commander reported to the United Nations that the tide of battle had turned and that the backbone of the North Korean Army was broken. On November 3, operations were in progress to destroy all North Korean forces. Then came the flood of

Chinese Communist "volunteers." Then came military disaster.

In retrospect, it appears that the Indian delegate's advice should have been heeded. Had the Chinese Communists come in anyway, the United Nations forces would have had a more defensible line at the waist north of the Thirty-eighth Parallel. A great victory was turned into a defeat. It took months for the United Nations forces to fight their way back to the Thirty-eighth Parallel.

When victory finally came, the United Nations was not prepared for peacemaking. When the Seventh Assembly met in resumed session in August, 1953 to set up a political conference to make peace, it was anticipated that most of the members of the United Nations would have a sense of achievement because aggression had been defeated by the collective will of mankind. A new list of martyrs, members of the United Nations armed forces, had been added to those who throughout history had struggled for freedom.

However, to everyone's consternation there was disagreement as to who should represent the United Nations at the conference. Would it be a round table conference or a conference of two sides? The focal point of the argument was India. It was the wish of over half the members of the United Nations, but not two-thirds, that India should be at the conference. The United States opposed India's participation, partly because of Syngman Rhee's violent objection. It argued that only those nations which had fighting forces in Korea were entitled to sit at the political conference and that other members were, in effect, neutrals. This concept did not give sufficient recognition to the fact that the United Nations had collectively resisted aggression, that forty-four had voted Communist China an aggressor and that almost forty members had supplied material aid.

Naturally, the nations lost interest in Korea except for

the sixteen which had fighting forces there. They lost the vision of this greatest effort of collective security. It may well be that the restricted point of view as to who was entitled to be represented at the peace conference gave a powerful impetus to the movement for neutralism.

Retreat from Collective Security

Since the Korean fighting ended there has been a retreat from the principles of collective security. The Collective Measures Committee established by the Uniting for Peace Resolution has held no substantive meetings in the last five years. However, it should be pointed out that the Committee during its first two years made some important recommendations for collective action in the future. The United States played an important role in this Committee and suggested it study the possibility of a United Nations legion.

The reasons for the retreat are numerous. There has been general disappointment over the failure of the United Nations to conclude the Korean affair decisively. United Nations forces are still maintaining an armistice line approximating the Thirty-eighth Parallel. The Peiping government and its North Korean puppet regime refuse to agree to a United Nations goal for the unification of Korea. The large and disproportionate American casualties have resulted in the Korean fighting being referred to in the United States as a war in which the United States was engaged rather than collective action under the United Nations. A shining example of collective security has been dimmed for immediate history.

The bipolarization of the world into the Western and Soviet blocs, which made the enforcement of collective security difficult in 1950, has been accentuated in the last five years. No combination of forces could be great enough to stop an aggressor supported by one or the other of these atomic giants. This bipolarization of the world has caused an increasing number of members of the United Nations to elect neutralism. By 1960, twenty-four states had been admitted to the United Nations since the beginning of resistance at the Thirty-eighth Parallel in Korea. Of these members, those from Asia and Africa particularly are anxious to avoid taking sides between the atomic giants.

This is not to say that the consciences of more than two-thirds of the members of the United Nations would not be touched again by another aggression and would not respond. Nevertheless, the chances are less likely that two-thirds would declare a nation the aggressor as they did when Peiping intervened in the Korean fighting. The moral issues would have to be clearly presented if the overwhelming number of members were to be found willing to supply material aid against the aggressor, as they were in 1950.

However, in the perspective of history, the United Nations action at the Thirty-eighth Parallel may well have saved the United Nations from going the way of the League of Nations. Frequently, the judgment of history supports the righteousness of a first instinctive action.

In comparison, review the prewar years! In the tragic years of the late thirties before the outbreak of the Second World War, there was a chain of aggressions. When these aggressions could be permitted no longer and resistance was necessary, war was inevitable. The chain of aggression might have been interrupted if the nations had acted to save Austria or Czechoslovakia. It was too late to save Poland without war. It may very well be that the verdict of history will show that United Nations resistance in Korea interrupted a chain of aggressions that might have led to a Third World War.

The principles of collective security are sound. The world cannot have peace without such a system. There must be universal law against aggression. Judgment must be given through proper legal procedure. There must be an obligation on the part of the nations to take action against the aggressor. Chapter VI will deal with what steps have been suggested to re-establish United Nations collective security.

Regional Security Arrangements

Various states, including the United States, have turned toward regional security arrangements as an alternative to a universal system of collective security. American Secretaries of State have frequently pointed out the large number of multilateral and bilateral arrangements to which the United States is a party as indicating American participation in a wide system of collective security. Indeed, the United States has military arrangements of some kind or other with some forty states. These do not include the collective security obligations which the United States has to eighty-one other members of the United Nations.

The Charter obligates the parties to any dispute to attempt to seek settlement by a variety of methods including ". . . resort to regional agencies or arrangements. . . ." Two articles of the Charter are specifically a source of regional arrangements—Articles 51 and 52. Strictly speaking, Article 51 contains no provision for a permanent regional arrangement. It was a perfectly logical development, nevertheless, that security agreements such as the North Atlantic Treaty Organization be based upon it. Indeed, Article 51 provides an interesting example of Charter evolution. This Article recognizes the right of individual or collective self-defense pending action by the Security Council. The Article itself has furnished a way around the Security Council veto by the use of the General Assembly. In the United States, this use of Article 51 was advocated from two different quarters. In 1946, it was put forward by the American Association for the United Nations. It was also put forward by Hamilton Fish Armstrong, Editor of *Foreign Affairs*.

Article 52 of the Charter contemplates regional arrangements created to settle disputes and deal with problems within the region. The Organization of American States has such a purpose. Obviously, the European nations bound together in the Atlantic Pact are developing a great deal of regional machinery, from the peaceful use of atomic energy to a guarantee of human rights. These regional functions have followed rather than preceded the security agreement. The other regional arrangements, such as the Southeast Asia Treaty Organization, and what was originally called the Baghdad Pact, etc., are regional alliances and lack machinery for the settlement of disputes within the region.

What has frequently been referred to by the United States as collective security arrangements have been military alliances. They lack third-party judgment and the other elements of true collective security.

The picture, however, is not as negative as has been painted. Since Korea the United Nations has taken action which stopped military intervention. It has held emergency sessions of the General Assembly. It has created an international force called UNEF. It has established a new international concept called a United Nations "presence." In other words, the United Nations has functioned in what might be said to be an area between the procedures of Chapter VI and Chapter VII.

UN Emergency Action in 1956

The two crises in 1956 already alluded to are illustrations. The United Nations showed brilliant improvisation in utilizing new methods to maintain peace and stop fighting without resorting to the formal charge of aggression.

At no time in the history of the United Nations have two

great Western powers been subject to such world-wide criticism as were Britain and France when they invaded Suez. Their invasion was branded a violation of the Charter. To the nations that had recently been freed from colonialism, an ultimatum and a military landing in Africa seemed like a repetition of colonial enterprises of a bygone day. Although discussions in the General Assembly indicated a greater sympathy for Israel, the delegates nevertheless demanded the withdrawal of Israeli troops.

The British, French and Israelis, responding to an appeal of world opinion in the United Nations, agreed to withdraw their troops as a United Nations emergency force took over. The General Assembly gave the Secretary-General seventy-two hours to recruit this emergency force. This he did in thirty-nine, with the able assistance of Dr. Ralph Bunche, Andrew Cordier and others. A United Nations official made a series of telephone calls in about the following order: a call to certain Scandinavian countries stating that the United Nations was ready for their contingents for UNEF and that they would be called for that afternoon; a call to the Pentagon asking that the air transports the United States had promised be in the countries designated that afternoon; a call to the Italian government to have a landing field ready where the United Nations troops were to shape up; a call to the Swiss government requesting Swiss Air to stand by to carry the troops from Italy to Suez; a call to United Nations authorities on the spot in Suez reporting the troops could be there within forty-eight hours.

The General Assembly instructed the Secretary-General to clear the Suez Canal. He recruited vessels from various countries and the Canal was cleared in advance of the target date.

In comparison, the simultaneous emergency session to

secure the withdrawal of Soviet troops from Hungary was a disappointment. The Soviet Union was not responsive to public opinion as were the British, French and Israeli governments. United Nations action is not only dependent upon how well it can mobilize world public opinion, but upon how well its members respond to it. Russia has never recovered the lost confidence of both Europe and the new states as the result of her defiance of the United Nations.

The Assembly's moral position is clear. With the UN membership in 1956 of seventy-seven members, the resolution demanding Soviet withdrawal of troops from Hungary was passed by a vote of fifty-four for, with eight against and fifteen abstentions. And in 1959, the Fourteenth General Assembly with eighty-two members again deplored the Soviet refusal to comply with Assembly resolutions by the following vote: fifty-three for, ten against and seventeen abstentions.

In the examples of Suez and Hungary, Chapter VII was not invoked formally to condemn a nation as the aggressor. And yet the United Nations certainly acted beyond the machinery for the peaceful settlement of disputes contained in Chapter VI. In other words, the United Nations has operated in an area stronger than the peaceful settlement of disputes but less strong than collective measures for the prevention of aggression.

The UN "Presence" Appears

The Middle East produced another crisis two years later. In 1958, a combination of meetings of the Security Council and the General Assembly clarified the situation there. In response to a request for action by the government of Lebanon, which claimed its frontiers menaced by Syria, the United Nations sent observers to the Lebanon-Syrian border. Later, feeling that the force of observers was not adequate, the government of the United States landed troops in Lebanon at the request of the Lebanese government, and immediately notified the Security Council. Simultaneously, British forces landed in Jordan. The Security Council held a number of meetings at which the Soviet Union demanded the withdrawal of American and British forces. The UN observers reported they had not been able to find a massive infiltration of the Lebanese frontier which the Lebanese government claimed.

At this moment, Mr. Khrushchev agreed to a summit conference. The governments of the United States, Britain and France replied in favor of such a conference if it were to be held under the United Nations. Mr. Khrushchev agreed and then made a quick visit to confer with Mao Tse-tung. After this visit, he reversed his original suggestion for a summit conference and proposed an emergency session of the General Assembly instead. At this Assembly, the influence of small states—the third force, so to speak—was well illustrated. The Soviet delegate tabled a resolution which could not pass. Friends of the United States tabled a resolution which, although it would have passed, would have registered so many abstentions as not to represent the moral authority of the General Assembly. Whereupon ten Arab states produced their own resolution, which was passed by the General Assembly unanimously. This resolution provided that the Secretary-General take such practical arrangements as would "adequately help to uphold" the purposes and principles of the Charter in relation to Lebanon and Jordan under the present circumstances.

On the basis of this resolution, the Secretary-General established a United Nations "presence" in Jordan.

Conditions in the Middle East are far from stable, but they are vastly improved. At the present time, the United Nations has three types of presence in the Middle East:

UNEF, the Israeli-Arab mixed armistice commissions and the Secretary-General's personal representative in Jordan.

In the fall of 1959 there was a combined action of the Security Council and the Secretary-General to preserve the independence of Laos. The government of Laos appealed to the United Nations, claiming that her frontiers were menaced by Communist guerrillas coming in from North Vietnam. It was suggested in the Security Council that that body send a fact-finding mission to Laos. Article 29 authorizes the Security Council to establish such subsidiary bodies as necessary for it to perform its functions. Thus a fact-finding body could be sent by the Security Council under this article of the Charter.

Presumably, to establish such a body was a procedural matter and could be done by any seven votes of the Security Council. The USSR invoked the double veto by claiming the decision as to whether or not a matter was procedural or a substantive decision was vetoable. The Security Council overrode the claim of the Soviet Union to the double veto. It decided by a simple majority that sending a fact-finding body to Laos was procedural and consequently sent such a body. The report of the group that went to Laos was inconclusive. The import of its conclusion, however, was that reports of infiltration had been exaggerated. However, the unresolved problem of infiltration remained. Again, the Secretary-General moved to fill the vacuum.

The Role of the Secretary-General

The expanding role of the Secretary-General has been one of the most important developments in the peaceful settlement of disputes. It has resulted from courage and wisdom on the part of the first Secretary-General and his successor, a liberal interpretation of the Charter, and the existence of certain vacuums which the General Assembly and the Security Council have asked the Secretary-General to fill.

The authority of the Secretary-General stems from Chapter XV of the Charter. The Secretary-General ". . . shall act in that capacity in all meetings of the General Assembly, of the Security Council, of the Economic and Social Council, and of the Trusteeship Council, and shall perform such other functions as are entrusted to him by these organs." And he may ". . . bring to the attention of the Security Council any matter which in his opinion may threaten the maintenance of international peace and security."

The first sentence of Article 97 provides that "the Secretariat shall comprise a Secretary-General and such staff as the Organization may require." The first liberal use of this article was by Trygve Lie. At one time, because of necessity and by bold improvisation, he had recruited a force of some seven hundred guards, radio technicians, chauffeurs, automobile mechanics and others to accompany United Nations missions in the field. Someday this group may be called the beginning of a United Nations peace force.

At the emergency meeting of the Security Council in 1950, Trygve Lie, using his authority under Article 99 of the Charter, called the attention of the nations to a breach of the peace at the Thirty-eighth Parallel in Korea.

Earlier in 1950, Trygve Lie formulated ten principles of peace to be accomplished in twenty years. One of them suggested that the question of Chinese representation in the United Nations be dealt with decisively, a step which in retrospect many people, including Americans, wish had been taken then. Trygve Lie journeyed from New York to Washington to London to Paris to Moscow to present his ten principles to the major governments.

Under Dag Hammarskjold's administration, the role of the Secretary-General has been further expanded. Time and again, Mr. Hammarskjold has dared to visit various capitals to seek a reduction of tensions or a settlement of disputes. He has traveled widely to encourage nations in the fulfillment of their United Nations obligations and to find out how the United Nations could help. In the winter of 1959-60, Mr. Hammarskjold concluded an extensive visit to Africa. There he undertook to find out what were the most effective steps the United Nations should undertake to fulfill its objectives of a dynamic international society on behalf of the nations struggling for freedom or who had just attained it.

The Secretary-General has been asked frequently by United Nations bodies to undertake missions and to make settlements on the spot which could not be spelled out by the General Assembly. He was asked to visit Communist China to secure the release of United Nations prisoners of war. He was asked by the General Assembly to recruit a United Nations force at the time of the Suez crisis and to clear the Suez Canal. He was authorized to establish a United Nations presence in the Middle East.

When the Subcommittee on Laos reported inconclusively the Secretary-General undertook to visit that unhappy country himself. He established a United Nations presence in the person of an expert who not only was to observe political conditions in the territory, but was to suggest a program of economic development. The result has been that Laos has moved to a degree of neutrality, with the agreement of the government of the United States. And it is generally assumed that the United Nations presence has the tacit approval of the Soviet Union.

Much of this success has been due to the genius of the present Secretary-General, assisted by an exceptionally able staff. He himself warned in early 1960, however, that there was a limit to what the nations could expect of his office. He warned that the powers could not dodge their responsibilities of meeting certain problems in the Security Council or the General Assembly.

The question is sometimes asked, would this genius be inherent in any successor? Mr. Hammarskjold has created a role which will greatly influence the choice of a successor. It is hoped that the initiative which he has taken will result in sufficient precedent, technique and tradition so that the enhanced role of the Secretary-General will continue even if another one has less vigor, wisdom and imagination.

Space does not permit a review of all of the disputes with which the United Nations has had to deal. At most, this chapter has indicated achievements and development of the United Nations peacemaking machinery, the problems facing a collective security system in a bipolarized world, and the expansion of the role of the Secretary-General.

III

DISARMAMENT

The Fourteenth General Assembly may have taken a very historic step in the movement for disarmament in a resolution sponsored by the unprecedented number of all the members of the United Nations. Adopted by the same number, it set general and complete disarmament under effective international control as the goal of disarmament negotiations.

Mr. Khrushchev of the Soviet Union made an address which contributed to the establishment of the final goal. The day before the Soviet Premier spoke, Selwyn Lloyd of the United Kingdom presented a disarmament program which, if fully carried out, would approximate total disarmament. Mr. Lloyd proposed disarmament in three stages, with controls beginning with the first stage. Ironically, it was Mr. Khrushchev's speech that crystallized the objective of a world without armies, without navies, without air forces, without military training schools, without weapons of any kind. Nothing would be left but a local constabulary with limited arms. Many delegates, feeling that there was a deep propaganda move back of Mr. Khrushchev's speech, may have resented the historic importance which will be credited his address.

No one believes that such a complete disarmed state of international society can be achieved within four years, as

the USSR Premier suggested. It may take many times that
number of years to achieve it. The statesmen found much
to criticize in the Soviet Union's detailed plan. In it, the
system of controls and inspection would only begin with
the fourth stage. No nation will proceed to disarm step
by step without clearly enunciated controls.

For some years, nations have talked about effective arms
control, limitations of armaments, phased disarmament, disarmament by stages, etc. It was logical for each nation to
present a partial disarmament program which would limit
that category in which its potential enemy is best prepared,
while being most reluctant to reduce that category which it
feels is most important for its security.

The resolution of the Fourteenth General Assembly
linked the phrase "under effective international control"
with the phrase "general and complete disarmament." The
final sentence of the resolution expresses the hope that
measures leading toward the goal of general and complete
disarmament under effective international control will be
worked out in detail and agreed upon in the shortest possible
time. The discussion in the Assembly gave the phrase "under
effective international control" a new meaning. The phrase
indicates more than inspection and machinery to see that
nations remain disarmed. It now describes a dynamic international order based upon law and with comparable peace
power.

The head of the United States Mission to the United
Nations, Henry Cabot Lodge, made an historic contribution to the goal of final disarmament. He said that if there
were general disarmament there would need to be "institutions to preserve international peace and security and to
promote the rule of law." He proposed the study of three
questions:

1. What type of international police force should be established to preserve international peace and security?
2. What principles of international law should govern the use of such a force?
3. What internal security forces, in precise terms, would be required by the nations of the world if existing armaments were abolished?

Secretary of State Herter on February 18, 1960 emphasized these points in an address before the National Press Club in Washington, D.C.

One by one various nations in the Fourteenth Assembly caught the spirit of the occasion. Many of them urged immediate steps that should be taken before total disarmament could be achieved. Many of them cautioned the length of the road before the final goal was attained. However, all of them accepted the final objective, which was sponsored and passed unanimously by the General Assembly.

The Assembly resolution provided that the discussions in the General Assembly and the declarations of the United Kingdom and of the Soviet Union be transmitted to the United Nations Disarmament Commission. This Commission, it will be remembered, is now composed of all the members of the United Nations. The Assembly further requested the Secretary-General to make available these documents for the consideration of the ten-nation disarmament committee to meet outside of the United Nations.

Sixty-One Years of History

The movement for disarmament can be said to have lasted, so far, for sixty-one years—that is, if one believes that it began with the suggestion of Czar Nicholas II of Russia that a peace conference be held at The Hague in 1899. The Czar was worried about the rising tide of armaments. Military men, particularly from the German Empire, succeeded in blocking any effective steps toward the reduction of arms. A world court was proposed at the conference but not set up because the nations could not agree on how the judges were to be selected. The most that could be agreed upon was the establishment of the Hague Court, consisting of a panel of judges from which nations seeking arbitration could draw arbitrators. Neither did the second Hague conference meeting in 1907 make any progress toward disarmament. The forces were already massing for the First World War.

More practically, however, one might say that the disarmament movement began with the League of Nations. This was the first effort to make disarmament and collective security part of the processes of organized community life. From the beginning of the League of Nations there has been a debate as to which comes first, collective security or disarmament. The classic point of view has been that nations will not give up armaments until they find in collective security the orderly processes of the international community. Individuals on a frontier are only persuaded to give up their guns if the community has adopted law with a sheriff to enforce it and a justice of the peace to administer it. So it is with nations.

More recently, armaments in themselves have been considered a source of instability. While it is logical to argue that nations will not give up their arms until they have another system of security, it is also logical to say that the arms of a few nuclear giants have reached such a stage that they work against the achievement of political security. Consequently, more and more the thought is that security and disarmament must come hand in hand.

Covenant and Charter Compared

Since the modern movement for disarmament began with
the League of Nations, it is worth comparing the League
of Nations Covenant and the United Nations Charter on
these subjects. The Covenant was more precise on disarmament and the Charter is more precise on collective security.
The United Nations Charter contains surprisingly little on
disarmament compared to the League of Nations Covenant.
The obligations of the League Covenant on disarmament
were more positive and binding. Article 1 (2) of the Covenant
made willingness to accept arms regulations a price of membership. In addition to giving guarantees of its sincere intention to observe its international obligations, an applicant
"shall accept such regulations as may be prescribed by the
League in regard to its military, naval and air forces and
armaments."

The Covenant recognized the influence of armaments on
peace when it said in Article 8 (1) the Council shall "formulate plans for such reduction for the consideration and
action of the several Governments." The Covenant further
provided that such plans would be subject to reconsideration
and revision at least every ten years. Article 9 provided for
a permanent commission "to advise the Council on the
execution of the provisions of Articles 1 and 8 and on military, naval and air questions generally."

On the other hand, the United Nations Charter neither
places disarmament as one of the overriding tasks of the
organization nor does it make willingness to agree to disarmament regulations a price of membership. The word
"disarmament" first appears in the Charter under Article 11.
This Article states that the General Assembly "may consider the general principles of co-operation in the maintenance of international peace and security, including the
principles governing disarmament and the regulation of

armaments, and may make recommendations . . . to the Members or to the Security Council or to both."

Under Article 26 of the Charter the Security Council shall be responsible for formulating, with the assistance of the Military Staff Committee, plans to be submitted to the members for the establishment of a system for the regulation of arms. Article 47 provides for the establishment of this Military Staff Committee, which shall advise and assist the Security Council "on all questions relating to the Security Council's military requirements for the maintenance of international peace and security, the employment and command of forces placed at its disposal, the regulation of armaments, and possible disarmament." Apparently the regulation of armaments was considered feasible—disarmament "possible."

What is the reason for the difference in emphasis? The First World War, the first to be waged with what then seemed the weapons of modern science, had shocked mankind. The Central Powers were disarmed, the Austro-Hungarian Empire fragmentized. The Soviet Union was not considered a military power. Disarmament agreement among the heavily armed states—the United States, the United Kingdom, France and Japan—seemed feasible. Indeed, in retrospect, disarmament appears so much easier then than now that one wonders why the League did not succeed in achieving it. One will always wonder whether if an arms agreement had been reached German rearmament could have been blocked, thus avoiding the tragic history of the postwar years, with the final catastrophe of the Second World War.

The League of Nations disarmament efforts failed because of the futility of striving for technical agreements while ignoring the necessity of a political agreement which would furnish a guarantee against aggression. For Americans the latter days of the decline of the League of Nations were tragic indeed. As James T. Shotwell has said, the United States pushed disarmament by mathematical ratio while ignoring at all times the need for collective security. Renunciation by Germany of the arms agreement of the Treaty of Versailles and her subsequent withdrawal from the League of Nations, were steps leading to the final collapse.

However, one should not discount the seriousness of the disarmament steps of the League of Nations. The late Major General George V. Strong said that the technical work of the League of Nations proceeded very far. General Strong was Chief Military Adviser to the United States Delegation during the greater part of the League of Nations Disarmament Conference. He stated shortly after the atomic bomb was dropped that the technical phase of the League's work, essential to the preparation of any disarmament convention, was of permanent value and, in fact, so far completed that not more than three months would be required to bring it up to date. General Strong died when the atomic bomb was quite new. His statement was made as scientists and military men were crossing the threshold of thermonuclear weapons.

The framers of the United Nations Charter profited by the lessons of the League. They placed collective security first. A series of collective security articles reached their climax under Article 43, by which the members agree to make available to the Security Council armed forces and assistance for action against an aggressor.

It would be a mistake to give the impression that disarmament was not in the minds of the framers of the Charter. However, the fate of the world for the next years seemed to be in the hands of the four or five big policemen with permanent seats in the Security Council. If they remained united, they could keep the peace of the world during the reconstruction period. They could agree among themselves on a reduction of armaments, both for themselves and for other nations. The building of the organization, therefore, and the establishment of a system of collective security seemed to be the first concern of the founders. Consequently, while the first disarmament obligation of the League of Nations Covenant is to be found in Article 1, that of the Charter is to be found in Article 11, and then in less positive terms.

However, between the time that the Charter was completed at San Francisco and the Organization was set up, the security provisions of the Charter were thrown out of balance. The United States ushered in the atomic age by dropping two bombs on Japan. Secretary Dulles, referring to this situation, said in part: "As one who was at San Francisco in the spring of 1945, I can say with confidence that had the delegates at San Francisco known we were entering the age of atomic warfare, they would have seen to it that the Charter dealt more positively with the problems thus raised."

Since the Charter was drafted fifteen years ago, the arms race has moved at a fantastic pace. Two phrases illustrate it. One is "nuclear deterrent." This phrase is used to describe the necessity of the atomic giants remaining at peace because in the attack and instant retaliation both would be destroyed. The other phrase is "operation overkill." This phrase indicates that state of preparedness where a nation goes on building beyond that which would be necessary to destroy its adversary.

In the fifteenth year of the United Nations there are two nuclear giants, each armed with enough nuclear weapons to destroy all life on the planet. Britain has belonged to the nuclear club for some time without making much of an effort to rival the stockpiles of the two giants. France, for prestige purposes, has entered the nuclear club. Communist China may enter shortly. One of the reasons pushing the United States, the Soviet Union and the United Kingdom to an agreement on the cessation of nuclear tests at Geneva is the fear of the greater anarchy that would result if many nations had the secret of atomic weapons.

The First Phase Negotiations

The first phase of disarmament lasted from the establishment of the Atomic Energy Commission down to the moment when the Soviet Union announced it had exploded an atomic bomb. The world had entered the atomic age between the time the San Francisco Conference adjourned and the meeting of the General Assembly in London in the winter of 1946. The very first resolution of the First General Assembly was the appointment of an Atomic Energy Commission at the suggestion of the United States, the United Kingdom, France and the Soviet Union.

Then the United Nations moved to the United States. One can picture the dramatic scene when the Atomic Energy Commission, composed of the members of the Security Council plus Canada, sat around the horseshoe table in the temporary Security Council room at Hunter College, New York City. Bernard Baruch was speaking. He presented the plan of the United States for the regulation and control of atomic weapons. It was an amazing plan indeed. Mr. Baruch proposed that an International Atomic Development Authority have a monopoly on the world's production of atomic energy, the Authority to have exclusive control of all atomic activities from the mining of raw material to the production and use of fissionable fuel. In addition to owning and managing all uranium and thorium mines, refineries, chemical separation plants and reactors, it was to have exclusive authority to engage in atomic research. The atomic energy authority could punish the individual or the nation for violation of the atomic energy agreements without a great power veto interfering. At this historic moment, the United States made the most far-reaching and dramatic proposals for supranational authority that any government has ever presented anywhere. It amounted to world government in a very important field of human activity.

The Soviet representative rejected the entire plan as "thoroughly vicious and unacceptable." The Soviet Union adopted the line then that it has consistently followed ever since: Outlaw atomic weapons, with a bare minimum of international control. Undoubtedly, the basic Soviet objection to the Baruch plan, although not presented in so many words, was that under it the United States would forever be the only power knowing the secrets of nuclear weapons. The United States might scrap all of its nuclear weapons. All peaceful atomic plants might be operated by the United Nations. But in the Russian mind, the United States would always have the advantage of having the experience of making the bomb. Russia's growing pride demanded that it, too, make bombs before they could be renounced.

The Second Phase

The second phase of disarmament negotiations began when the United States ceased to have a monopoly of atomic bombs. It was announced at the Fourth General Assembly that the Soviet Union had exploded a bomb. Nuclear rivalry was then accelerated. In 1952, the United States announced that it had achieved the hydrogen bomb. The race continued through the development of guided and intercontinental missiles. The Soviet Union announced that it had launched its first Sputnik into the orbit of the earth. The

United States followed with its Explorer. The Soviet Union placed a satellite into the orbit of the moon and photographed the opposite side of that body. The United States launched a satellite into the orbit of the sun.

In discussing all disarmament proposals, the Soviet Union has consistently opposed any lessening of the veto power. The United States and other nations have opposed the use of the veto in the question of inspection controls. Along with fear of the abolition of the veto is the Soviet fear of international inspection. Consequently, for a great number of years the Soviet Union has repeated the propaganda slogan "Abolish the bomb" without fully agreeing to the principle of inspection. In Russia a built-in suspicion of having other people see what is going on antedates the Communist regime. The fear of observation from outside goes back to the history of Czarist days. The Soviet Union at first accepted the principle of inspection, but insisted that each power do its own inspecting. Gradually it has accepted the principle of inspection and control to a certain degree, the major concessions being at the conference for the cessation of nuclear tests.

Disarmament Commissions

Various disarmament commissions have functioned in the United Nations. The first was the Atomic Energy Commission. It was followed in 1947 by the Commission for Conventional Armaments, also composed of the eleven members of the Security Council, plus Canada when not a member of the Security Council. American and Soviet attitudes toward the two commissions shifted as advantages swung from one side to the other. So long as the United States was the sole possessor of the atomic bomb, the Soviet Union wished one commission to consider both conventional and mass destruction weapons. When the Soviet Union achieved the bomb, it wanted a separation of the two functions, and the United States reversed its position and wanted both to be discussed by the same body. Obviously there was little in the way of disarmament negotiations during the Korean fighting, from 1950 to 1952.

In 1952 a new Disarmament Commission with the same membership took over the functions of the two. In 1954 a subcommittee of this Commission was appointed, consisting of four permanent members of the Security Council: United States, USSR, United Kingdom and France, plus Canada. Observers have said the fourth and fifth sessions of the subcommittee were the most intensive and serious periods of disarmament negotiations.

One would not want to give the impression that in the many meetings of the Disarmament Commission of twelve and its subcommittee of five nothing was done. A vast number of proposals came from all of the members. The basic problems seemed to be twofold. The cold war became more serious. Technical developments moved so fast that proposals for disarmament could not keep up with them.

In 1958, the Soviet Union rejected the idea of the twelve-power Disarmament Commission or the subcommittee, in which it claimed to be overwhelmingly outnumbered by allies of the United States. The Russians countered with a proposal for a larger commission composed of Western powers, Communist powers and neutrals. Despite the fact that India, sponsor of the resolution, accepted the proposals, the Soviet government then rejected the enlarged commission. The Soviet government's next proposal was for a Disarmament Commission to be composed of representatives of all of the members of the United Nations. This Commission had one meeting on the eve of the Fourteenth General Assembly.

In the meantime, two Geneva conferences were proposed,

one to formulate an agreement against surprise attacks and the other an agreement to suspend nuclear tests. The conference on surprise attack was proposed by the United States as an answer to Soviet charges before the Security Council that American planes, loaded with nuclear bombs, were flying far north to the Soviet frontier. This conference achieved no major results and adjourned fairly quickly. On the other hand, the conference for the cessation of nuclear tests was spurred on by a tremendous moral and emotional spirit that emanated from all of mankind.

In the former conference, possibly only a few of the great powers seemed to be immediately concerned with the danger of surprise attack, but all men fear contamination from nuclear tests. And the fears are justified, because in some parts of the world the air has been saturated to a dangerous degree from fallout. Some inhabitants in the American Pacific trust area were seriously affected by fallout from the American tests in the Pacific.

Another reason pushing the Americans, British and Russians to agree to a cessation of nuclear tests is the fear that other nations might start experimenting with atom bombs and join the nuclear club. It may very well be that Soviet fear of Communist China having nuclear bombs has much to do with the fact that she seems at times to be even more anxious than the nations of the West to suspend nuclear tests.

As this is written, at the beginning of the summer of 1960, the conference has gone on in Geneva for eighteen months and seems on the verge of achieving a result. It seems possible to reach an agreement to suspend nuclear tests aboveground and in the air. Both sides are close to an agreement on inspection and control. As for tests below ground, there is uncertainty as to the ability of sci-

entists to detect them. Consequently, it has been proposed
that there be a moratorium for a period of time on underground tests, during which scientists from both sides can
conduct experiments in monitoring underground explosions.

The Ten-Nation Committee

Reference has already been made to the fact that the Disarmament Commission met for a few brief hours preceding
the General Assembly of 1959. At this meeting, the representatives of the United States, the United Kingdom and
the Soviet Union submitted a proposal from the foreign
ministers' meeting recently adjourned in Geneva. The foreign ministers had been meeting to consider the possibility
of a summit conference. Their only accomplishment was
to suggest that a ten-nation disarmament committee consider what could be done to make a fresh start on the
problem. The committee was to be composed of five members of the Atlantic Pact and five members of the Warsaw
Pact. Consequently, representatives from the United States,
the United Kingdom, France, Italy and Canada were to
meet with representatives from the Soviet Union, Czechoslovakia, Poland, Bulgaria and Romania.

There were two major criticisms of such a committee.
First, it contained no representatives of Asia, Africa or Latin
America. There was no representation of that great part of
the world which would suffer along with the atomic giants
if a nuclear war were to start. In the second place, the
committee was not a committee of the United Nations.

It seemed to be another bit of evidence of the consistent
by-passing of the United Nations by the great powers in
1959. The United States government explained why it
had agreed to this conference outside of the United Nations. Since the conference is a parity one with five Western

and five Communist states meeting without any representation from the rest of the world, the United States does not want to establish a precedent for such a conference within the United Nations.

After the Summit Catastrophe

On the eve of the summit conference scheduled for May, 1960, the desire for disarmament seemed so overwhelming that it rather than the question of Germany appeared to be the one item on the agenda on which progress could be made. Indeed, it was hoped that early in the summit conference a dramatic announcement could be made of an agreement for the cessation of nuclear tests. Then came catastrophe. The summit conference ended before it began.

It is too early in the summer of 1960 to indicate how far back into the cold war the nations have retreated. Will Mr. Khrushchev's six to eight months' apparent truce on Berlin be followed by another blockade?

Today, after the break-up of the summit conference, where do the disarmament negotiations stand? The conference for a cessation of nuclear tests grinds on. The conference of ten blew up abruptly with the Soviet bloc stalking out of the meeting on the eve of the presentation of the revised Western plan. The Soviet Union has announced its intention of having a full-dress debate on disarmament at the Fifteenth General Assembly. The United States anticipates a meeting of the United Nations Disarmament Commission, which is made up of all the members, on the eve of the General Assembly. Possibly two facts have so far prevented the collapse of the conference for a cessation of nuclear tests. There is world-wide public opinion for a test ban. Neither side wishes to offend this public opinion by being responsible for the adjournment of the conference.

Furthermore, after eighteen months of dogged negotiations, the conferees were close to an agreement before the summit conference collapsed.

As for the ten-nation conference, it resumed under great difficulties. The two comprehensive plans, the Eastern and the Western, were presented to the conference. (Or, it should be said in the case of the Western plan that it was presented after the Soviet bloc walked out.) Shortly after the ten-nation conference resumed, the Soviet Union presented a revision of its plan for total disarmament which it had presented to the General Assembly. The plan did contain some important advances in that it accepted machinery for disarmament controls as an integral part of the United Nations and accepted the Western thesis that there must be a peace force. However, the Western powers felt that the Soviet delegate kept repeating again and again his demands for acceptance of the Soviet program for total disarmament without being willing to negotiate on the Western position that disarmament must proceed from one tested step to another. The Western powers also felt that the Soviet schedules for disarmament would be greatly to the disadvantage of Western security. For illustration, strategic bases would be given up in the first stage.

The four Western colleagues of the United States on the committee felt that the West should formulate its disarmament proposals in a more comprehensive and dramatic way. This was done. Although the Soviet delegates knew of the imminence of the Western proposals they withdrew from the conference and thereby terminated it without giving the West an opportunity for its presentation.

Quite obviously, the United Nations Disarmament Commission or the General Assembly will have both plans before it.

How far has the movement for disarmament been set back? As far as the spirit of good will and accommodation is concerned, it has been set back seriously. The spirit of Camp David, which was to make serious disarmament possible, has been followed by a general deterioration of East-West relations. Once again nations are reminded of the fact that unless there can be a reduction of tensions any reduction of arms is impossible.

On the other hand, as far as the long-range aspect is concerned, the movement for disarmament is ahead of where it was when the Fourteenth General Assembly opened in September, 1959. "General and complete disarmament under effective international control" is the final stated goal of eighty-two nations, members of the United Nations. Apparently all powers, including the Soviet Union, accept the fact that there must be a disarmament agency in the United Nations and there seems to be some move toward a UN peace force.

Furthermore, the words "control" and "inspection" have taken on a new dimension. To many people, these words now indicate something more than technical arrangements. They project a world of law, with adequate police force and the United Nations vastly strengthened to keep the peace.

Disarmament is an area in which public opinion can play a very important role. Public opinion has kept alive the nuclear test ban conference, despite the reluctance of atomic energy agencies and military departments of various governments. Overwhelming realization of the total tragedy confronting mankind if nuclear war should break out is forcing governments to continue disarmament negotiations on a broader and broader scale. The cost in waste, perverted energy, and indeed human liberty is becoming unbearable. A great part of mankind unable to defend itself does not relish being forced to take sides in a world bi-polarized by atomic giants. It is becoming increasingly distrustful of the capacity of these giants to keep their arms under control. Just as nuclear destruction would be world-wide, public opinion for disarmament is world-wide. It knows no frontiers.

IV

INDEPENDENCE, FREEDOM
AND HUMAN RIGHTS

The United Nations is concerned with human rights for the individual and freedom for the nation.

A plaque on the wall of a conference room in the Fairmont Hotel in San Francisco declares:

> 25 April–26 June 1945
> In this room met the Consultants of forty-two national organizations assigned to the United States Delegation at the Conference on International Organization in which the United Nations Charter was drafted. Their contribution is particularly reflected in the Charter provisions for human rights and United Nations consultation with private organizations.

It marks a historic meeting. Crowded into this room on May 2, 1945 were the members of the United States Delegation, headed by Mr. Stettinius, and the consultants. The latter presented a letter signed by many of them asking that the Charter contain additional and stronger phrases pledging the nations to respect human rights and fundamental freedoms. The author of this book was very anxious that the Charter provide for a commission on human rights. He was afraid that otherwise postwar reactions might prevent creating such a commission. Dramatic speeches were made by the consultants. Mr. Stettinius in his report to the President said that it was the intervention of the consultants that resulted in the provision for the Commission on Human Rights.

Obviously, the delegates from other countries, supported by their people at home, likewise wished the Charter to be strong in its provision for guaranteeing human rights and fundamental freedoms. They had seen the origins of the war grow out of the violation of these freedoms in Germany and Italy.

Freedom from fear was among the peace objectives stated in the Atlantic Charter. This declaration, signed by Prime Minister Winston Churchill and President Franklin D. Roosevelt in 1941, contains a remarkable phrase of nineteen words, only one of which has more than one syllable. It could be recommended to English classes as a classic of Anglo-Saxon. The clause reads ". . . that all the men in all the lands may live out their lives in freedom from fear and want."

Four years later, the second paragraph of the Preamble of the United Nations Charter pledged the nations ". . . to reaffirm faith in fundamental human rights, in the dignity and worth of the human person, in the equal rights of men and women and of nations large and small. . . ." And the third purpose stated under Chapter I contains the following clause: ". . . and in promoting and encouraging respect for human rights and for fundamental freedoms for all without distinction as to race, sex, language, or religion. . . ."

No part of the Charter better illustrates the obligations which the members take for both individual and collective action than the human rights provisions. Article 55, as has been pointed out, gives the United Nations as an organization obligations to promote human rights. Article 56 declares, "All Members pledge themselves to take joint and separate action in co-operation with the Organization for the achievement of the purposes set forth in Article 55."

These responsibilities, collective and individual, were vigorously illustrated in the action of the Security Council on March 30 and April 1, 1960, in condemning violence growing out of apartheid in South Africa. The Security Council made it clear that a nation cannot take protection in Article 2 (7) and declare its violation of human rights is a matter of domestic concern.

The Economic and Social Council is the body under the Charter which implements the human rights obligations. This body may prepare draft conventions in this field for submission to the General Assembly. It may call international conferences. And lastly, the Economic and Social Council has an obligation which the author and others fought for at San Francisco. Article 68 provides that it ". . . shall set up commissions in economic and social fields and for the promotion of human rights. . . ."

The protective arm of the human rights provisions of the Charter is extended to the peoples of the world who do not enjoy self-government. Under Chapter XI, members of the United Nations who have assumed responsibility for the administration of non-self-governing peoples accept as a sacred trust the obligation to assist these peoples in the progressive development of their political institutions. And under Chapter XII, establishing the international trusteeship system, one of the obligations of the trust powers is ". . . to encourage respect for human rights and for fundamental freedoms for all without distinction as to race, sex, language or religion. . . ." Inhabitants in the trust areas have the right to petition the Trusteeship Council for redress of grievances.

The International Labor Organization, which antedates the United Nations by several decades, may mark one of the first substantial references to human rights on an international level. Its Constitution declares that world peace is dependent upon international social and economic justice.

Similar obligations concerning human rights are reflected in the constitutions of other specialized agencies.

The Universal Declaration of Human Rights

The operating heart of the United Nations machinery for the promotion of human rights is the Commission on Human Rights. Mrs. Franklin D. Roosevelt was its first chairman. It was decided early that the Commission should produce an international bill of human rights. The bill was to be divided into three parts. The first was to be a declaration of human rights containing fundamental principles to which all peoples could aspire. The second was to be a covenant stating in treaty form those obligations of the declaration which could be so stated, ratified and become part of international law. The third part of the bill was to contain machinery for enforcement.

The first one of the three has been achieved. It was near midnight on December 10, 1948 when the General Assembly, meeting in Paris, adopted the Universal Declaration of Human Rights. The delegates had before them the draft text of the Declaration. The text represented two years of discussion and deliberation in meetings of the Commission. The Declaration was adopted by forty-eight votes in favor, none against, and eight abstentions. Before its adoption, Mrs. Roosevelt stated that the Declaration was first and foremost a declaration of the basic principles to serve as a common standard for all nations. It might well become the Magna Carta for all mankind.

The wording of the Declaration lacks the moving drama of the American Declaration of Independence or the French

Declaration of the Rights of Man, because the United Nations document had to be translatable into five different languages. Granting this handicap, it reads amazingly well.

When the Declaration was adopted, the President of the General Assembly said: "It is the first occasion on which the organized community of nations has made a declaration of human rights and fundamental freedoms, and it has the authority of the body of opinion of the United Nations as a whole, and millions of men, women and children all over the world many miles from Paris and New York will turn for help, guidance and inspiration to this document." The record will show that his prediction was correct.

Covenants Not Yet Completed

The statesmen anticipated that work would start on the second part of the international bill of human rights, the covenant on human rights. Indeed, John Foster Dulles, one of the United States delegates to this historic Assembly, so predicted. Over ten years have passed. The nations have not yet completed the second task. The statement of human rights in treaty form has shown itself to be a more formidable task than anticipated. There early developed a difference of opinion between the older democracies and the new states. The former thought of a covenant on human rights in terms of the basic civil rights which are part of the Western system of justice. The newer states wished to place equal or even greater stress on economic rights. Many people able to speak as equals for the first time spoke from the background of hunger and misery. The right to eat and the right of a man to support his family are basic human rights.

While the Western powers were sympathetic to the latter point of view, they doubted that it could be expressed in an international treaty. The economic conditions of many states vary greatly. They vary from prosperity to poverty, from industrialization to extremely primitive means of support. Under such conditions, it is difficult to draft a treaty guaranteeing the right to a job or to social security.

A compromise was reached. It was decided to draft two covenants, one on civil and political rights and one on economic, social and cultural rights. The Commission on Human Rights met in sessions for about six years to formulate the two covenants. It then passed them on to the General Assembly. For a number of years, the General Assembly through its Third Committee has been debating the two covenants.

The Secretary-General said that it is not surprising that the drafting of the two covenants has taken so long. Between them, he said, they ". . . cover almost the whole of the relations between the individual and society, something which, as recently as a generation ago, was considered as coming within the exclusive domestic jurisdiction of states."

The enthusiasm for completing the two covenants was chilled in 1953 when the American Secretary of State said that the Administration would not submit them to the Senate for ratification when completed. It is ironical that the Secretary was Mr. Dulles, who in 1948 had said that the Declaration should be followed by a binding covenant. Mr. Dulles also declared the United States would not press at the moment for ratification of the Genocide Convention. Neither would it sign the Convention on the Political Rights of Women. It is assumed that the Department of State's renunciation of the human rights covenants was an effort to persuade the Judiciary Committee not to report the Bricker Amendment favorably to the Senate. This amendment would have seriously limited not only the authority of the President to make executive agreements but the authority of the Senate to ratify covenants.

At each General Assembly, the Third Committee continues to debate and accept additional clauses to the two covenants. Eventually, they may be completed and ready for ratification. However, the whole task of writing two covenants has shown itself to be so formidable that there are those who believe it may be necessary in the long run to draft a whole series of covenants. Each one would deal with a specific human right, which could be put into treaty form and ratified.

Influence of the Declaration of Human Rights

In the meantime, the cause of human rights has been unexpectedly advanced through the Declaration. This Declaration, despite the fact that it was never to be ratified, has grown to have greater and greater influence. It has been so widely utilized in human rights discussions that many authorities, including the Secretary-General, have stated that it has become a source of law.

Various resolutions of the General Assembly have been based upon its principles. The texts of many of its articles have been incorporated into peace treaties, trust agreements and the constitutions of new states. It has been cited as an authority by domestic courts. The member states are expected to use the Declaration as a standard in giving their reports each three years on the condition of domestic human rights.

The European Convention for the Protection of Human Rights is based upon the Universal Declaration of Human Rights. This document was signed on the fourth of November, 1950 by the foreign ministers of thirteen European states. The Convention represents a significant contribution to the cause of human rights by the Council of Europe. Its Preamble refers to the Declaration of Human Rights ". . . proclaimed by the General Assembly of the United

Nations on 10 December 1948. . . ." The Convention then states, "Being resolved, as the Governments of European countries which are like-minded and have a common heritage of political traditions, ideals, freedom and the rule of law, to take the first steps for the collective enforcement of certain of the rights stated in the Universal Declaration . . ."

The influence of the Declaration goes on. Its principles tend to become part of the common law of nations.

Other Human Rights Agreements

Another human rights convention was adopted by the General Assembly and submitted to the members for ratification —the Genocide Convention. The word genocide was coined to describe what the Nazis attempted to do—to destroy a whole people on the basis of race, culture and religion. As of April, 1960, sixty-two governments had deposited instruments of ratification or accession. But so indiscriminate has been its opposition to conventions in the human rights field that the United States, which loudly condemned the crime of genocide, has refused to ratify it. Clearly the General Assembly in 1959 could have condemned as genocide the Chinese conduct in Tibet. It was revealed as an effort to destroy the religion, the culture, if not the life of a people. However, because the government of the United States had not ratified the Convention, it could not make the charge.

In 1955, the United Nations proceeded to draft a new antislavery convention. It found some so-called "refined" forms of slavery that had not been covered by the original League of Nations antislavery convention, which the United States had ratified. The United States would not serve as a member of the drafting committee to produce a new convention. It would not ratify it.

A study of United Nations reports on the work in the

field of human rights lists among others the following subjects: prevention of discrimination and protection of minorities; refugees and stateless persons; protection of trade union
rights (freedom of association); forced labor; slavery and
servitude; plight of survivors of Nazi concentration camps;
missing persons; prisoners of war; status of women, followed
by political and economic rights of women, status of women
in private law, nationality of married women, status of
women in the trust and non-self-governing territories. The
women of the United States, particularly those who have
stood for the equal rights of women throughout the world,
cannot help but be chagrined at their country's refusal to
ratify conventions on the rights of women.

Despite general opposition to human rights covenants,
the United States government agreed to support the effort
of the International Labor Organization to draft a convention on forced labor. The treaty is now in effect, thirty-one
ratifications having been deposited. The U. S. Government
has not pressed for ratification.

When the government of the United States declared that
it would not submit the human rights covenants to the
Senate for ratification, it abdicated any chance to influence
the completion of these documents to satisfy the views of
the American people.

However, the United States quickly moved in the Commission on Human Rights and the Economic and Social
Council for a different type of program for the promotion
of human rights and fundamental freedoms. In this, the
United States government has been successful.

The U. S. Action Program

In 1953, the American representative on the Human Rights
Commission, Mrs. Oswald B. Lord, submitted the United
States Action Program. This program consisted of three

parts: the first, a program of periodic reports on human rights; the second, a series of studies on human rights; the third, technical assistance in certain human rights fields.

The first part of the program provided that governments of states which are members of the United Nations and specialized agencies are asked to submit reports to the Human Rights Commission every three years. These reports are to describe developments and progress achieved and the measures taken to safeguard human liberty in metropolitan areas and in non-self-governing and trust areas. Again, the influence of the Declaration of Human Rights is shown. The reports are to be based upon the principles enumerated in the Declaration. The reports shall also be based upon the rights of peoples to self-determination. The new states have insisted that human rights agreements recognize this right.

Forty-one governments submitted the first triennial reports covering the years 1954-1956. The Commission on Human Rights does not sit in judgment on a particular nation. It rather studies the reports in order to give to the Economic and Social Council a picture of human rights conditions throughout the world and recommendations for their improvement.

The second part of the program is to comprise a series of studies on specific rights. Considerable progress has been achieved. The program provides for a series of studies on discrimination: in education, religious rights and practices, occupation and employment, political rights, and emigration and travel. They are to be carried on under the auspices of the Human Rights Sub-Commission on Prevention of Discrimination and Protection of Minorities. In each case so far, the studies have resulted in proposals for a standard of conduct by governments and individuals to be incorporated in the form of either recommendations or conventions or both. And when the subject of the study falls within the area of a specialized agency, that body is asked to participate in the drafting of the required document. For illustration, the International Labor Organization produced a convention on discrimination in employment. The problem of discrimination in education was turned over to UNESCO. That body will consider whether to adopt a recommendation or convention at its General Conference in November of 1960. The Sub-Commission is now working on religious rights and political rights. It will be seen that in the new program the United States government has not been able to avoid international conventions completely.

Fortunately, the Sub-Commission was meeting in 1960 when quite unexpectedly there were manifestations of anti-Semitism throughout the world, accompanied by such symbols as swastikas. The world was disturbed at the sudden manifestation of prejudices long thought uprooted, and members of the Sub-Commission were swept to unexpected action. The International League for the Rights of Man proposed that the Sub-Commission undertake a wide inquiry into the facts, causes and remedies. Other organizations so urged. Consequently, the U. S. member took the initiative in forming a plan for such an inquiry which was adopted unanimously. The resolution adopted calls upon governments, private ogranizations and UNESCO to submit information on recent manifestations of anti-Semitism, racial prejudice and religious or racial hostilities of a similar nature, which have occurred in various parts of the world and portend danger to the cause of human rights. The Action Program on Human Rights proposed by the United States has moved forward.

On March 31, 1960, the Security Council gave a vigorous reaffirmation of the fact that the clauses of the Charter to advance human rights and fundamental freedoms are affirmative, binding obligations. Human rights are not matters exclusively for domestic concern. Various representatives, including that of the United States, on the Council made effective statements which were considered a strengthening of United Nations law on the subject of human rights.

On the United Nations' fifteenth birthday, the human rights score might be described as follows: The Universal Declaration of Human Rights was adopted quickly. It has had unexpected influence. The process of agreeing about the covenants on human rights is much slower than anticipated. Certain conventions, such as the political rights of women, genocide, forced labor, antislavery, etc., have had substantial ratifications, except for the noticeable absence of ratifications by the United States. It is anticipated that the governments will comply with requests for reports each three years on how well they are carrying out the principles of the Declaration. The various studies on discrimination in various phases of activity, such as employment, education, etc., have produced concrete results.

As for the score on national observance of human rights, there still remains a considerable portion of the world where a knock at the door at midnight strikes terror into human hearts. There remains a large area where basic civil rights such as freedom from arbitrary arrest or freedom of speech are almost unknown.

Freedom for the Nation

The independence of colonial peoples is closely allied with human rights and fundamental freedoms.

Seven hundred million people, almost one-third of the world's population, have won their independence since the United Nations Charter was drafted. This has been called history's greatest social revolution. Africa a few years ago was considered the last place in the world where peoples would demand freedom quickly. Now the desire for freedom is sweeping the "dark continent." Within a few years at least twenty additional sovereign states will knock on the door of the United Nations for admission. The membership of the Organization will then have increased to over one hundred.

The seeds of this independence were sown in the Second World War. Obligations to grant independence or self-government were planted in the Charter. Undoubtedly, many nations would have demanded independence under any circumstances. However, the United Nations and the provisions of its Charter have made the difference between nations seeking independence in a world of anarchy and their seeking independence within the orderly framework of international society. It is not too romantic a figure of speech to say that the United Nations has beckoned these nations to membership. And it welcomes them into the fraternity of the Organization.

Such independence, however, is not an automatic guarantee that human rights will be safeguarded by the new governments. All of the constitutions of the new states incorporate principles of the Universal Declaration. However, the effort to translate these principles into practice will be for Africa as for the rest of the world a matter of constant effort and education.

War, its suffering, its artificial prosperity, its friendly or unfriendly invasion of soldiers, touched every part of the world. The colonial world could not slumber after its experience in the Second World War. The delegates anticipated this awakening. They wrote into the Charter obligations to advance self-government and independence which they undoubtedly would not have agreed to in some of their reactionary moods following the war.

Specifically, non-self-governing peoples are dealt with in Chapters XI, XII and XIII of the Charter. Under Chapter

XI, headed "Declaration Regarding Non-Self-Governing Territories," the members assume wide obligations for the administration of territories whose people have not yet attained a full measure of self-government. The very phrase "have not yet" is prophetic. Under this same chapter, each ruling power is ". . . to transmit regularly to the Secretary-General for information purposes, subject to such limitation as security and constitutional considerations may require, statistical and other information of a technical nature relating to economic, social and educational conditions in the territories for which they are respectively responsible other than those to which Chapters XII and XIII apply."

Over the objection of some of the colonial powers, the General Assembly established a committee to assess these reports regularly submitted to the Secretary-General. If reports were to be submitted to the Secretary-General, some body should assess them. Why not the General Assembly?

Roads to Independence

The United Nations early played an important part in the granting of independence to colonial areas. The first legislative act of the General Assembly was to exercise authority conferred upon it by the treaty of peace with Italy in which it was to dispose of the Italian colonies, if the great powers should fail to agree over such disposal. Of course, the great powers did disagree and the General Assembly set the terms for eventual independence of Libya, Eritrea and Somaliland. When the British surrendered their Palestine mandate, the General Assembly filled the vacuum by assuming authority to determine the fate of the area. After reviewing the report of its subcommittee, the Assembly agreed to partition of Palestine and the establishment of the state of Israel.

Other colonial areas have achieved their independence through a more liberal policy on the part of the colonial powers. The United States gave the Philippines their independence in 1946. The British recognized the right of the subcontinent of India to partition and the two parts to become independent. India and Pakistan elected to remain members of the British Commonwealth.

One of the most amazing tributes to the British people occurred in the General Assembly in 1957, at the time the Federation of Malaya was admitted to the United Nations. One by one, members of the British Commonwealth rose to pay tribute to the United Kingdom for granting independence to another part of its empire which had elected to become a member of the Commonwealth. Other members of the United Nations joined in the tribute, the majority speaking English. One was aware in this inspiring moment that the tight little island of Great Britain with its principles of justice and freedom has spread its influence throughout the entire world. Many members of the United Nations are members of the British Commonwealth or have otherwise severed ties with Great Britain and become independent since the Second World War ended.

France has been much slower to adjust herself to the movement for independence. However, a year ago, General de Gaulle offered independence or membership in the French Community to all of the French territories in Africa, except Algeria.

As for Algeria, the French for some time insisted the territory was part of the French Metropolitan area. But in 1959, General de Gaulle promised Algeria a choice between integration, independence or membership in the French Community after a settling-down period of five years. However, the fighting in that unhappy land goes on. The problem of Algeria has been brought before the General Assembly repeatedly by the former colonial territories. It will arise to plague the French until a solution in freedom is found.

One French territory, Guinea, elected independence in 1958. It was immediately admitted to the United Nations. This fact set in motion a chain reaction among practically all of the French territories to ask for independence so that they, too, could join the United Nations. The French constitution has been revised, so that nations that choose independence may enter the United Nations and may remain associated with the French Community. This general reaction set off by admitting Guinea to the United Nations is said to account in part for General de Gaulle's present coolness to the world organization.

Chapters XII and XIII establish the international trusteeship system and the Trusteeship Council. The trust areas are to be first of all the old League of Nations mandates. It will be remembered that at the close of the First World War territories taken away from Germany and Turkey were placed under the League of Nations mandates system. These territories were divided among some of the Allies, who were to be the mandatory powers. The first obligation of these powers was the well-being of the native inhabitants. They were also to prepare the people in the mandated areas for self-government. When these territories were ready, they were to be given freedom. It was the first world recognition of responsibility for dependent areas.

In addition to the League of Nations mandates, the United Nations trusteeship system would include territories which might be detached from states as the result of the Second World War and territories voluntarily placed under the trusteeship system.

When the Union of South Africa refused to transfer her mandate to United Nations trusteeship, the General As-

sembly sought an advisory opinion of the International Court
of Justice. The Court advised that since the Union of South
Africa would not transfer its mandate to the trusteeship
system, its government must continue to administer the territory under the terms of her League of Nations mandate.
In other words, the obligation to the world community for
the administration of this area could not be escaped.

The trusteeship system is being rapidly liquidated. British
Togoland voted in a United Nations plebiscite to join with
the Gold Coast to make the new state of Ghana and as
such has become a member of the United Nations. French
Togoland became independent in April, 1960. It will likewise seek admission to the United Nations. The trusteeship
for the French Cameroons has been liquidated and a new
state, Cameroon, will be admitted to the United Nations
by the Fifteenth General Assembly.

The Charter of the United Nations did not anticipate the
rapidity of the movement for independence. Consequently,
it did not provide for an orderly reduction in size or the
eventual disappearance of the Trusteeship Council. Under
the Charter, this Council is to be composed of the members
administering trust territories, the permanent members of
the Security Council and as many other members elected to
the Trusteeship Council as may be necessary to insure an
equal balance between administering powers and nonadmin-
istering powers. So many trusteeships have been liquidated
that the Council should now be reduced in size. In fact, its
entire existence may be unnecessary within a few years unless
new trusteeships are added.

Ironically, the only trust areas that may remain a few years
after 1960 may be the United States trusteeship for the old
Japanese mandated islands and the Australian trusteeship
for New Guinea. The former embrace some sixty thousand
indigenous people scattered over islands that dot an area

of the Pacific as great as that of the United States. And yet if all of these islands were put together, they would not make a land mass larger than the state of Rhode Island. Obviously, these scattered sixty thousand people cannot become a viable state. They can, however, become self-governing under the United States and thus be freed from trusteeship.

The Challenge to the Mature Powers

The rapid movement for freedom of the dependent peoples presents the United Nations and its members with great problems and great opportunities. The opportunities will outweigh the problems, if statesmen have imagination.

One could well have wished that freedom might have come to the colonial world, particularly the African part of it, more gradually and more orderly. Certainly one might wish that there had been more time for the preparation of these people for self-government. Freedom, however, does not necessarily come in a logical order. When a sentiment for freedom sweeps an area, it cannot be held back. Freedom cannot be rationed. People are going to have it whether they are ready for it or not, peaceably or explosively. And who should deny this right? These people in the twentieth century have the same right to declare themselves free and make their own mistakes as did the thirteen American colonies or the republics of Latin America.

Obviously, new states vary greatly in background, capacity and size. Some of them, such as India, have a heritage of hundreds of years of civilization from which they will make an important contribution to the fabric of international society. Other states are emerging from a tribal system, which, despite a complex form of organization, has less to contribute to modern society.

All, however, no matter how rich or primitive the background, share the status of the underprivileged. They do most of their work with their own hands. Many of their people are undernourished. Illiteracy is high. They do not have enough teachers for their schools.

As far as the African states are concerned, some of them have uncertain boundaries. The colonial powers were not necessarily careful to divide Africa ethnically or logically. Consequently, there will be a long period of bickering over frontiers. Many of the nations in Asia which have recently won their independence have long years of national memory. On the other hand, some of the new nations in Africa have no national sentiments beyond those of the tribe. Consequently, a spirit of nationalism and patriotism follows rather than precedes the desire for freedom.

Some of the units being carved out of colonial empires seem almost too small and limited in resources to make viable states. One may hope that the trend toward small independent states will eventually run its course and be followed by a tendency toward federation or union.

The development of the institutions of democracy in the new states may take years of evolution. In some of the new states, democracy has given way to a strong man, a dictator, who has become caretaker for the democracy. In some of the new states, a two-party system at present seems to have no meaning as one knows it in the older democracies.

Many of the nations lack trained native civil servants. The break with the past should be sufficiently orderly that the trained civil servants of the former empire remain. If they do not, some of the governments will have difficulty in finding enough trained men to run their fiscal systems or their courts. It is hard to picture the Belgian Congo, which received its independence on June 30, 1960, getting along without trained civil service, at least for some considerable time.

What does this have to do with the United Nations? First,

as has been seen, the United Nations had much to do with the independence of many of these states. Its Charter inspired all of them. Second, the entrance of these new members into the United Nations has a profound effect on the organization itself. And third, a very heavy responsibility rests upon the United Nations to help the new independent peoples to stability, freedom and a richer economic and social life.

The entrance of the new states will have a profound effect on United Nations bodies. In some cases, their entrance is having an effect on the attitude of the older members toward those bodies. Until development plans have had a chance to succeed, the United Nations will have a larger number of states proportionately which will have few resources to contribute to the world organization. Rather, they must call upon the United Nations for a speed-up of aid of all kinds.

However, the new states can make an important contribution to the maintenance of international peace and security. First, they must avoid violence among themselves and lean upon the United Nations for help in stabilizing their frontiers and settling their disputes. And the more advanced of them can become part of the growing third force that insists that the great powers co-operate.

Some of the older states are disturbed at the increase in the size of the General Assembly. Its membership in mid-1960 of eighty-two delegations will increase to over one hundred within two or three years. Now no great power, not even the United States, can be assured of a two-thirds majority of the General Assembly in favor of its proposals. Nor can it be certain that it may be able to garner one-third of the votes of the Assembly, plus one, to prevent an antagonist from getting two-thirds of the vote of the General Assembly against its wishes.

Physically, the United Nations headquarters will be more

crowded. One hundred members means one thousand delegates in the Assembly Hall and in the lounges. Several hundred experts will be added to this number. The architects are already examining the building to see how the facilities can be expanded to accommodate this considerable increase.

There will be a tendency for Assembly debates to be longer. A statesman from a country that has just won its independence will be more anxious for self-expression than a delegate from an older state.

But these are all obstacles that can be turned into steppingstones, if the older nations have imagination, understanding and judgment. As far as the physical and technical arrangements of the Assembly are concerned, the facilities can be expanded.

Chapter VI of this book anticipates permanent machinery for the General Assembly. It might be given year-round permanence through arranging for some of its committees to be in continuous session. Or several of the committees might meet some months in advance of a plenary session. Some way must be found for the Assembly to conduct the vast amount of business before it and to give full self-expression to all of its members, while at the same time insuring that the plenary sessions will be short enough to make it possible for foreign ministers and prime ministers to take major decisions.

The original members of the United Nations must realize that a world organization cannot be a comfortable club of like-minded people. No nation should wish the certainty of a majority in the United Nations. The United Nations should be a reflection of the entire world that exists. It may not be as easy to secure a two-thirds vote of the General Assembly. However, this fact is not an excuse for the great powers shying away from the General Assembly. Rather, they should strive to state their views so clearly and sincerely that they will be able to secure a two-thirds vote.

And they will find that wise policies, unselfishly expressed, will in the majority of cases be identified with an overwhelming vote of the members. For the United States, the United Kingdom and France, the situation provides a tremendous challenge and opportunity.

As for the United States, the blow that the American colonies struck against the colonial system in 1776 is having its final effect in the second half of the twentieth century, when most peoples will be free to have their own form of government. The new states will make serious mistakes. But the world was generally skeptical between 1776 and 1784 about the ability of the American colonies to organize their freedom and maintain an independent government. The final answer was not given until the conclusion of the Civil War several generations later.

As for the United Kingdom, a considerable portion of the membership of the United Nations recently have been freed from British colonial rule and are members of the British Commonwealth. They share a common heritage of British justice.

As for France, likewise a considerable number of the members of the United Nations that have recently been given freedom from the French Empire will remain associated with the French Community. They will be tied to France by many cultural and economic bonds.

Why should not these former colonial empires, now systems of commonwealth and community, see the important role that they can play in the United Nations in helping and guiding these new states? It is a role that they can play only in the United Nations.

Because so much of the help that the new states will need is in the economic and social field, the next chapter will discuss how the great powers can accept the challenge which these new states offer.

V

STANDARDS IN LARGER FREEDOM

One can imagine a cartoon picturing earth man roaming over the celestial bodies with Mother Earth shouting to him that there is plenty to do at home. While man is sending satellites into outer space as a prelude to celestial exploration, more than one-half of the people at home are hungry, cannot read or write, and are generally miserable. Although the situation might not be very logical, it is perfectly natural. It is human nature to reach for the stars before one solves the problem of the poverty about him.

The Fifteenth General Assembly of the United Nations has an agenda that reflects man's inconsistencies. It has a report on the peaceful uses of atomic energy and outer space exploration. But it also has a report from the Children's Fund describing the millions of hungry children who must be fed. It has reports from the Economic and Social Council and the specialized agencies that point up the fact that over a billion people in the world are considered underprivileged.

The economic problems confronting the United Nations have grown with the years. Economic problems tend more and more to become world-wide. Man's capacity for production becomes greater. Nevertheless, because increased production is felt first by the more industrialized nations, it can be said that the rich get richer and the poor get poorer. The disparity between the wealthier nations and the underprivileged actually has become greater rather than less. The number of people on earth increases so rapidly that the phrase "population explosion" is commonly used. A great part of the world has won its independence from the colonial system. It is experiencing a second revolution called "the revolution of rising expectations."

The United Nations has developed a considerable machinery to facilitate economic and social co-operation between all nations. Much of it is concerned with increasing cultural contacts and trade between the wealthier nations. But so pressing is the problem of the underprivileged peoples that many UN activities center on helping them.

One and One-Quarter Billion People

It is generally estimated that more than 1,250,000,000 people live in underdeveloped areas; and this figure does not count 650,000,000 in Red China who are proceeding to lift themselves by their own bootstraps. One of the most vivid descriptions of these areas is to be found in the excellent booklet written by Paul G. Hoffman, Managing Director of the United Nations Special Fund. It is entitled *One Hundred Countries—One and One Quarter Billion People*. Mr. Hoffman describes an underdeveloped country as follows:

> Everyone knows an underdeveloped country when he sees one. It is a country characterized by poverty, with beggars in the cities, and villagers eking out a bare subsistence in the rural areas. It is a country lacking in factories of its own, usually with inadequate supplies of power and light. It usually has insufficient roads and railroads, insufficient government services, poor communications. It has few hospitals, and few institutions of higher learning. Most of its people cannot read or

write. In spite of the generally prevailing poverty of the
people, it may have isolated islands of wealth, with a
few persons living in luxury. Its banking system is poor;
small loans have to be obtained through money lenders
who are often little better than extortionists. Another
striking characteristic of an underdeveloped country is
that its exports to other countries usually consist almost
entirely of raw materials, ores or fruits or some staple
product with possibly a small admixture of luxury
handicrafts. Often the extraction or cultivation of these
raw material exports is in the hands of foreign com-
panies.

Mr. Hoffman points out that the United Nations desig-
nates as "less developed" all countries and territories in
Africa, with the exception of the Union of South Africa;
South America; Asia, with the exception of Japan, Aus-
tralia and New Zealand. The United Nations estimates omit
mainland China, North Korea and North Vietnam, because
of the absence of statistical reports. Of the one and one-
quarter billion peoples on which the United Nations has
statistics, 70 per cent, or 838,000,000, have an average per
capita annual income of under $100; 208,000,000 have an
average per capita annual income of more than $100 but
less than $200; 73,000,000 have an average per capita in-
come of $200-$299. The United Nations lists a fourth group,
with an average income of $300-$699. It is composed of states
that are moving rapidly to escape the designation of "less
developed." These include Argentina, Lebanon, Puerto
Rico, Israel, etc.

Of the first list, the peoples with an annual per capita
income of under $100, twenty of them have won their politi-
cal independence since the Second World War began, and
they have joined the United Nations.

Three facts in this situation are outstanding. One is that

one and one-quarter billion people, not including Communist China, are miserably poor. The second is that they have been inspired to want a better life. The third fact is that the members of the United Nations have taken an obligation, individual and collective, to improve the lot of these people.

There are three types of aid being given to the underprivileged peoples at the present time. The largest amount of money is spent for the bilateral program in which one country gives directly of money and experts to another. The program of the United States, stemming from President Truman's Point Four speech, is the largest. The contribution of France to technical assistance has been confined primarily to Africa. France's per capita contribution is one of the largest bilateral programs of any of the great powers.

Another type of aid is regional. The best illustration of this is the Colombo Plan, in which the nations of South and Southeast Asia, largely members of the British Commonwealth, assisted by the mother country and the United States, have a considerable program of economic development.

For the purposes of discussion here, however, we are concerned with the third type, the multilateral. It centers primarily on the United Nations and the specialized agencies. There has been some effort recently to find a better term than "technical assistance." The word "technical" is hardly broad enough to cover all investment capital and industrial equipment. Also effort is being made to substitute "cooperation" for "assistance." However, for the purposes of this volume, it is better to use "technical assistance" as meaning economic development in the broadest sense.

Technical assistance in some form or other has a long history. The idea that one nation can draw upon the skills of another goes back to antiquity. Christian missionaries were forerunners of technical assistance programs to the ex-

tent that they brought medicine, education and other skills
to teach people how to live better lives.

The Rockefeller Foundation was an early pioneer in the
field of organized philanthropic technical assistance. Indeed,
the whole modern development of this concept had much
of its origin in the imagination of the late John D. Rockefeller, Jr. The Ford Foundation and other philanthropic
bodies have in various ways followed the example set by
the Rockefellers.

Helping less developed peoples to a better way of life is
like most sound programs—a combination of idealism and
self-interest. Possibly the two combine in "common interest."
Hugh Keenleyside, for twelve years director of the United
Nations technical assistance program, said that there was
abroad in the world a spirit of kindliness. He described it as
the program based upon a desire to help people help themselves. There is today the spirit of the missionary in thousands of men and women from some sixty-five countries who
go into other countries on programs of economic and cultural development.

UN Objectives

To show how the nations have co-operatively responded to
the spirit of kindliness, one has only to look at the program
of the United Nations and its various agencies.

The framers of the Charter planned a well-rounded organization whose work would provide, on one hand, for
the peaceful settlement of disputes and resistance to aggression. On the other hand, it would provide for the
removal of the causes of war by promoting human rights and
a better economic life for all people. And after the threat of
war has been reduced and the last colony freed, there will
remain as the United Nations' long-range task the promotion
of a better life for the peoples of the earth.

The stated purposes in the Preamble of the Charter emphasize that the organization is ". . . to employ international machinery for the promotion of the economic and social advancement of all peoples. . . ." Again: ". . . to achieve international co-operation in solving international problems of an economic, social, cultural, or humanitarian character . . ." and ". . . to be a center for harmonizing the actions of nations in the attainment of these common ends. . . ." Indeed, the clauses just quoted are not simply declarations of purpose. Under Article 2 (2), "All members, in order to ensure to all of them the rights and benefits resulting from membership, shall fulfill in good faith the obligations assumed by them in accordance with the present Charter." Thus there is the affirmative obligation to promote international co-operation in economic, social and humanitarian fields.

The Economic and Social Council, whose members are elected by the General Assembly, is the organ primarily responsible for the implementation of these principles and obligations. According to the Charter, it ". . . may make or initiate studies and reports with respect to international economic, social, cultural, educational, health, and related matters. . . ." It may make recommendations with respect to such matters to the General Assembly, to the members and to the specialized agencies. The Economic and Social Council calls international conferences in related fields.

It was the Economic and Social Council which appointed the Human Rights Commission. It has appointed other commissions. As the world has become more complex, this body of the United Nations has an increasing responsibility. It early elaborated a set of principles to guide the specialized agencies in their approach to the underdeveloped areas. The principles state:

The participating organizations should, in extending technical assistance for economic development of under-developed countries:

1. Regard it as a primary objective to help those countries to strengthen their national economies through the development of their industries and agriculture, with a view to promoting their economic and political independence in the spirit of the Charter of the United Nations, and to ensure the attainment of higher levels of economic and social welfare for their entire population. . . .

The UN Economic Family

A very large United Nations family of agencies of various kinds has developed. The majority of them, individually and co-operatively, function in the spirit of the above principles.

Most of the members of this family are called specialized agencies. There are twelve of them. Together these agencies touch almost every phase of human existence outside of political matters, which are the special provinces of the Security Council, the General Assembly and their political bodies. Because the United Nations family grew in a rather haphazard manner, it has been more difficult to co-ordinate their activities. Some of them either antedate the United Nations or came along with it. The rest developed through the years.

Many of the specialized agencies grew out of the League of Nations or other prewar organizations. The oldest major specialized agency is the International Labor Organization. It was created along with the League of Nations. It, of all the League of Nations bodies, survived the war intact. After living out the war years in exile in Montreal, it returned to its home in Geneva.

The Food and Agriculture Organization actually came

into being on October 16, 1945, eight days before the Charter was finally in effect. FAO grew out of the United Nations Conference on Food and Agriculture, which met during the war at Hot Springs, Virginia, in May, 1943. It has taken the place of the old International Institute of Agriculture in Rome. This is one reason why FAO is located in Rome.

The International Bank and Monetary Fund grew out of a conference at Bretton Woods, New Hampshire, in 1944. The Articles of Agreement actually came into force on December 27, 1945. The United Nations Educational, Scientific and Cultural Organization (UNESCO), which came into being on November 4, 1946, grew out of the work of the League of Nations Institute of Intellectual Co-operation. Paris became its home as it was of the old Institute. The World Health Organization is an outgrowth of the League of Nations Health Section. At the conference in San Francisco, a proposal was made for the creation of a specialized institution in the field of health. WHO officially came into being on September 1, 1948.

Other specialized agencies followed.

In addition, the United Nations has another body called the International Atomic Energy Agency. Technically, this is not a specialized agency, because it reports to the General Assembly first instead of through an agreement with the Economic and Social Council as is the case with the specialized agencies. Its origin and affiliation with the United Nations deserves special consideration here. This is an illustration of the General Assembly acting with authority and wisdom. And in functioning at its best, the Assembly was successful in modifying the wishes of the great powers. Furthermore, the Agency itself deals with the new scientific discoveries whose effects may be so great as to produce a second industrial revolution.

At the Tenth General Assembly the representative of the

United Kingdom and the United States reported that a committee meeting in Washington had produced a plan for an atomic energy agency. The United States government had just published the plan. Members of the United Nations were invited to send their comments and suggestions to Washington. The British delegate went so far as to say that his country did not believe that the General Assembly was the place to debate as highly technical a subject as atomic energy. Whereupon, the General Assembly proceeded to debate the subject and the plan. Small states felt that their collective judgment expressed through the General Assembly would carry more weight than a series of individual opinions expressed to Washington.

After some weeks of debate in which the delegates of smaller states demonstrated that they were able to speak on as complex a subject as atomic energy, the United States agreed to enlarge the drafting committee which was to meet in Washington. The United States further agreed that after the plan was revised, it would be submitted to a conference of members of the UN and the specialized agencies. At such time, there would be further chance to suggest revisions. As a result, a much better agency was created.

It is generally assumed that another agency for man's advancement will be one for outer space control. The composition of this agency will call for as much imagination as the subject with which it deals.

The United Nations has four bodies which are integral parts of the organization, rather than intergovernmental agencies. These are the United Nations Children's Fund, the Office of the United Nations High Commissioner for Refugees, the United Nations Relief and Works Agency for Palestine Refugees in the Near East, and the United Nations Special Fund.

The Expanded Program

In 1950 the United Nations adopted its Expanded Technical Assistance Program. Three major forms of technical aid are provided: (1) technically qualified experts, sent out at the request of underdeveloped countries to advise governments and train local staff in a wide variety of economic development fields; (2) fellowships or scholarships granted to enable nationals of underdeveloped countries to study modern methods in similar fields abroad, often in conjunction with the sending of an expert; and (3) the organization of training centers and seminars on a regional basis to enable experts of several countries to exchange ideas and experience in particular technical fields. In addition, a limited amount of equipment is provided for demonstration and teaching purposes in support of development projects.

Fifty-four governments pledged slightly over twenty million dollars for the 1950-1951 budget. Eighty-four governments pledged over thirty-one million dollars for the 1958 budget. It is truly a co-operative effort of many nations, in which the underdeveloped make some contribution, even though they will be recipients of the greatest amount of aid. Part of this money is used for the United Nations own technical assistance program. Part of it is used to pay the specialized agencies for undertaking projects. A Technical Assistance Board under the chairmanship of a United Nations staff member contains a representative of each of the specialized agencies. They examine requests for aid from member states. The money is contributed to those agencies who are best able to undertake a particular project.

An American recently returned from a United Nations technical assistance assignment in the Middle East had a team of persons working for him, only 10 per cent of whom came from the United States. Together they faced the following problems: There was the immediate problem of a food supply. The population was growing. What was the best diet for its people based upon what they could best raise? The health of the people was important. If malaria was eliminated more people could raise more food. What were the best routes of getting material to market and to the ports for export? The people in the villages badly needed basic education. They must understand more about the tools that were being provided them; they must be able to read the instructions. Their national accounting system was inadequate. Altogether six agencies of the United Nations combined to help a proud and courageous people, who have demonstrated their willingness to fight for freedom, develop economic and social strength.

Space does not permit an account of what each specialized agency contributes in the broad field of assistance to mankind. It is interesting that each agency represents a particular interest such as health, labor or aviation. Each thinks of world peace in its particular sphere of interest. This makes for a richness and variety of effort.

For illustration, the Constitution of the International Labor Organization states that world peace is dependent on international social and economic justice. The contribution of the ILO to the joint program is to advance social and labor standards in the areas that are being given technical assistance. The original purpose of the ILO was to bring together employees, employers and governments in an effort to improve labor standards by international agreement. The lowest standards were by international agreement to be brought nearer and nearer to the standards of the more prosperous nations. The International Labor Organization was one of the first international bodies to bring together representatives of private bodies on an equal level with representatives of government. Each delegation to a conference of the

ILO is composed of two representatives of the government, one selected by the leading labor organization in each country and one by the employers' organizations.

The entrance of Communist states, where independent employers are absent and labor is not free, has in the minds of some served to fog the principle of tripartite representation. However, the vast majority of the members of the ILO have a legitimate distinction between representatives of governments, of employers and of employees.

As time has gone on, the ILO has devoted relatively less attention to developing international agreements for the improvement of labor standards to be ratified by various governments. It has spent more time in assisting in the program of technical assistance to underdeveloped areas. It is natural that the ILO feel an important mission in this regard. Above all of the bodies, it should be most aware of child labor, sweatshops, slums and all of the unfortunate consequences of the first industrial revolution. The ILO feels a mission in helping avoid these conditions that might well accompany, and in some instances are accompanying, industrialization of underprivileged areas. Consequently, the ILO is ready to help a new country develop fair labor practices. Indeed, in some instances it actually trains workers for skilled tasks that need to be performed.

One of the specialized agencies which contributes greatly to the program of helping underdeveloped areas is the World Health Organization. Its Constitution states that the health of all people is fundamental to peace and security and is dependent on the fullest co-operation of individuals and states. In some parts of the world, United Nations is a household word. Almost everyone has seen trucks with the UN insignia carrying doctors and sanitation experts to combat disease.

The contribution which the Food and Agriculture Organization makes is to help people produce more and better food and to distribute it. Officials of the FAO believe that to eliminate hunger reduces restlessness. If the people have a better diet, they will be able to work harder. There is certainly a relationship between the two agencies. In one area of Pakistan, rice production increased 100 per cent because with the elimination of malaria the people could work.

It is not an exaggeration to say that there is, in a sense, a race between these two organizations. Lord John Boyd Orr believes that the population of the world will treble its present size before the increase is checked by the natural results of a higher standard of living. Can the food supply of the world keep pace with this increase in population? In other words, food producers and farmers can hardly find enough food to take care of the increasing population because of the success of the doctors and health experts.

The United Nations Educational, Scientific and Cultural Organization (UNESCO) might be said to be the educational division of the United Nations. It thinks of war in terms of lack of education and consequent ignorance. Its Constitution states that wars begin in the minds of men. Because it deals with the realm of the intellect, its programs have seemed more diffuse and sometimes too intellectual to practical people. It has in the last few years tended to find itself in the broad program of technical assistance. To put it very simply indeed, how can people use the tools given them unless they can understand the instructions? UNESCO is concentrating to a very great extent on basic education. The Director-General of UNESCO, returning from Latin America in the spring of 1960, said that UNESCO had succeeded in changing the system of basic education of some Latin-American countries.

UNESCO produced a human and instructive documentary film. The opening scenes show a Thai boy riding on his elephant and a Mexican boy riding on his donkey. The boys were very much alike in their simple desires for kindliness and fun. Despite different civilizations and historical backgrounds, the problems of disease and poverty and illiteracy were about the same. One might say that the ILO infuses social conscience and UNESCO the thirst for knowledge in the over-all technical assistance program.

Financing Development

The purpose of the International Bank is to loan money to governments for sound projects that will assure the repayment of the loans. The International Bank is the "toughest" of the specialized agencies. The total capital of the Bank amounts to $9,510,000,000 of which 20 per cent is paid-in capital. Sixty-eight countries are members of the bank. Each subscription is based upon relative economic resources. By May, 1959, the Bank had made 231 loans in forty-nine countries and territories totaling over $4,463,000,000. The bonds of the International Bank are purchased as good investments.

The nations were aware of a gap between technical assistance and the conservative loans of the International Bank. Under the technical assistance program of the United Nations and the specialized agencies, experts are sent to advise countries on the improvement of their economy, to study their transportation, to drain their swamps, to inoculate their babies and to spray their homes to eliminate malaria. What seemed to be needed to fill the gap was financial assistance for basic development projects. These projects are not self-liquidating and cannot justify loans from the International Bank or private investment. But they are so basic that without them undeveloped countries may not be far enough advanced to justify bank loans and private investment. The majority of poorer states advocated a Special UN Fund for Economic Development. It was commonly called

SUNFED. The Western powers, the United States and Great Britain, said that they could not contribute to such a fund until they could save money from disarmament.

Two approaches have been made to meet the problem. In 1958, a new dimension was added to the technical assistance program by the creation of the Special Fund. Its basic purpose was to make a survey of the resources of the world and the possibilities of economic development. Its budget was set at one hundred million dollars. Paul G. Hoffman, former Director of the Marshall Plan, was named its Managing Director. Consequently, for the first time, a world-wide effort is being made to know the resources and the possibilities of industrial development.

A second step is the creation of the International Development Association. This organization is a division of the International Bank. Its purposes are ". . . to promote economic development, increase productivity and thus raise standards of living in the less developed areas of the world. . . ." This is to be done by making loans on more flexible terms than the conventional loans of the International Bank.

Membership in the Association is open to the same countries that are members of the Bank. The IDA is closely affiliated with the Bank and therefore a specialized agency of the United Nations. Its initial capital will be one billion dollars. The United States' subscription to it will be 32 per cent. The seventeen industrialized member countries will pay their subscriptions over the five-year period in gold or freely convertible currencies. The fifty-one less developed member countries will pay only 10 per cent of their subscriptions in gold or freely convertible currencies; ninety per cent will be in their own currencies. Paul Hoffman estimates that the capitalization of only one billion dollars over five years is obviously too little to overcome the minimum investment gap of two billion dollars a year. But it is a beginning.

Two of the most humanitarian divisions of the United Nations are the United Nations Children's Fund (UNICEF) and the Office of the United Nations High Commissioner for Refugees. The Children's Fund began as an emergency organization. When its continuing need was recognized, it was established as a permanent body. It has succeeded in feeding millions of children and giving them medical assistance.

The United Nations High Commissioner for Refugees is trying to keep ahead of the number of refugees, but man's inhumanity to man produces them about as fast as he can settle the older ones. The problem of European refugees will be almost solved at the end of World Refugee Year. Most of the camps in Europe will have been reduced or closed. But the stream of refugees from Tibet into India is still coming. World Refugee Year, which ran from July 1, 1959 through June 30, 1960, may have accomplished much to focus the attention of the world on the seriousness of the refugee problem and to raise more money for clearing more camps.

The Economic and Social Council has four economic commissions—one each for Africa, Asia and the Far East, Latin America and Europe. This last made an effort to develop East-West economic co-operation at a time when the division between the two parts of Europe was very sharp. Delegates who have sat on the Economic and Social Council are quick to point out that one of the most successful and practical operations of the system has been the functioning of these regional economic commissions. Each nation feels that it has a particular responsibility and authority in developing the commission in its own area.

The Problem of Co-ordination

How much co-ordination shall there be between the United Nations and the specialized agencies? This is an increasingly important problem. The agencies are highly autonomous. There is obviously an advantage in having separate agencies in that each brings experts from a particular field. The total result is a richness of personal contributions. However, there would seem to be a need for closer co-ordination to make a massive assault on the problem of the underprivileged.

The Secretary-General in his address dedicating the buildings of the University of Chicago Law School on May 1, 1960 pointed out two tendencies. One was the desire to create a new organization for each task which the United Nations undertook. Possibly the process of proliferation will stop with an agency for outer space and one for disarmament. The time may have come to strengthen existing machinery rather than adding new bodies.

The Secretary-General also pointed out that each agency was quite independent in its relationship with the others. At the same time, practically all members of the agencies are members of the United Nations. The Secretary-General (referring to this independent relationship) went on to say: "At least it seems to me that, if this tendency is accepted and continued, it should be counterbalanced by an effort to evolve new forms for integration of the work of the various international agencies." Presumably the Secretary-General was expressing his disappointment that the agencies had not agreed to co-operation in a bold program for economic development in Africa. The considerable sums of money and technicians required for a bold program must dictate closer co-ordination.

Under the Charter, the Economic and Social Council may co-ordinate the activities of the specialized agencies through consultation with and recommendations to the General Assembly and its member nations. The Economic and Social Council does not have the authority to command a higher degree of integration of program. It can, however, make strong recommendations to the member states. Their influence could be felt on the agencies themselves.

Co-operation Instead of Competition

How much aid should be given through the United Nations and how much bilaterally? This is the most important problem in the technical assistance field confronting the United States and the wealthier states.

It is the unanimous testimony of representatives of the underdeveloped areas and the new states that they would prefer to receive aid through the United Nations. They give the following reasons:

When these states receive aid through the United Nations, they are not forced to choose sides in a power struggle. One nation in Africa found it could no longer count on its former colonial ruler for technical assistance. It found that the Soviet Union was willing to fill the vacuum. Obviously, the country in question would have preferred to have been able to make a direct plea for an expanded program through the United Nations. The new countries are anxious to avoid having to choose sides between the atomic giants for fear that they must become committed to one side.

In the second place, they feel that they can receive in dignity aid from an agency in which the new states share the controls. The small states are members of the economic and social committees of the General Assembly. They elect members of the Economic and Social Council. They make up the membership of the economic commisssions for the various continents. Practically all of them belong to the specialized agencies as well, and share in the controls of these agencies. Consequently, they feel that they may take decisions for the development of an over-all program from which they receive help.

In the third place, the underprivileged states may contribute something themselves. They may contribute technicians, money and ideas. In 1958, 1,187 technicians were drawn from sixty-four countries and sent to one hundred political units. It may very well be that Ghana or India or Israel may develop a particular skill, say in irrigation, and be able to contribute it to another underdeveloped area. It is sometimes said that a citizen of India can better understand the problems of Thailand than a citizen of one of the Western countries who has not shared the common misery of the underdeveloped. Most of the nations that receive technical assistance contribute something, even if it is only a few dollars of their own currency, to the technical assistance fund. Each year a pledging conference is held. The contributions may vary from a few dollars in its own currency from Cambodia to a large contribution from the United States. Some states which do not contribute to the United Nations budget contribute to the Expanded Technical Assistance Program and the Special Fund.

The new states may contribute ideas to the common pool of technical knowledge for the aid of the underprivileged. The ideas of many nations go into the technical staff of the United Nations and the specialized agencies.

From the standpoint of the more prosperous nations, the program under the United Nations goes farther for less money. The recipient powers contribute housing facilities, etc. for missions in their countries. It is estimated that the total contribution of the recipient countries is larger than the total technical assistance budget.

Finally, it has frequently been said that the United Nations is the only sponsor of a development program that can afford to say "no." Frequently, great powers are afraid to turn down a project submitted by another state because there is always the implied threat that help might be secured from another power. When the United States withdrew its support from the Aswan Dam for various reasons, Egypt turned to the Soviet Union. The United Nations assesses programs entirely on their merits. It is able to say "yes" or "no" based upon the soundness of the program.

Three arguments are frequently advanced for the United States' giving as much aid as possible directly: It is suggested that if the United States gives the money directly it can control the funds; the recipient countries will know definitely where the money comes from; the United Nations does not have machinery to administer a program involving as much money as the United States bilateral program involves. A comparison between the efficiency of the United Nations program and the American bilateral program certainly is not to the disadvantage of the United Nations. Since all recipient countries participate in the direction of the United Nations program, they will know very well where the aid comes from. And as far as the machinery for a program is concerned, the United Nations has a very considerable machinery of its own and through its specialized agencies, capable of unlimited expansion.

The United States is proposing that its NATO partners join with it in a greater effort to aid the underdeveloped areas. However, it would be a mistake if separate machinery were created for this effort. It would duplicate United Nations machinery. The new states are aware that many of the members of NATO are the former colonial powers. It would be tragic if sharper competition developed between the Soviet bloc and the Western bloc in giving aid outside the United Nations.

Africa should be a showcase in which all of the wealthier states, including the former colonial powers, co-operate through the United Nations, its Special Fund and the specialized agencies in one great effort at economic and social co-operation. The African continent lends itself particularly to such a program. The new states and those about to be free need help on a vast scale. Shall Africa be open to a new type of economic colonialism, in which the Western powers and the Soviet Union compete with each other in order to win her allegiance in a power struggle? Or shall Africa receive aid through the United Nations?

The program suggested does not mean, of course, that some nations would not contribute more than others. Presumably the United Kingdom, France and the United States would make the largest contributions to such an aid program. Quite obviously, the former colonial powers wish to safeguard their investments in their former colonies. However, the new states in Africa, sensitive to "colonialism," will welcome a bold program through the United Nations.

The United Nations established the Economic Commission for Africa in the spring of 1958. There are fifteen members of this Commission. In 1960 six of these are European countries with African colonies. Membership in the Commission is open to any state in Africa which may subsequently become a member of the United Nations. States that cease to have any territorial responsibilities in Africa cease to be members of the Commission. Any territory in Africa not yet responsible for its own internal or international relationships may, upon presentation of its application to the Commission by the member responsible for those international relationships, be admitted as an associate member, and there are nine associate members. Judging by the rapidity with which Africa is moving toward independence, there will be many more full members of the Commission in the very near future.

Secretary-General Dag Hammarskjold returned from a trip to Africa in the winter of 1959-60 imbued with the idea that Africa provided a tremendous challenge and opportunity to the United Nations. He immediately asked for an African development fund that would be the beginning of a greatly expanded economic program.

One could hardly have anticipated that in July, 1960 the Republic of the Congo would present the United Nations with one of its severest tests. This unhappy land called upon the United Nations for the widest possible range of help. It involved the sending of a considerable international military force to establish law and order. It involved emergency help with food and medical supplies. It involved long-range technical assistance because in that vast land not one doctor or engineer remained after the exodus of the Belgians. The Secretary-General warned the nations that they must be called upon for increasing sacrifices. He asked the Security Council to request the specialized agencies for every possible help in the United Nations program.

The Secretary-General has moved to establish a series of United Nations "presences" in Africa. These representatives can advise him as to what is needed and supervise the technical assistance programs being carried out there. It was anticipated that such a representative in any African country would be the symbolical presence of the United Nations, helping to establish stability in that area. And in the case of Dr. Ralph Bunche, who was fortunately in the Republic of the Congo when the rebellion occurred, he also was called upon to help supervise the operations of the UN force.

STRENGTHENING THE UNITED NATIONS

The startling changes that have come to the world since the Second World War ended foretell even more startling changes to come. Man looks into a future of outer space travel and is planning to land on celestial bodies. His population is increasing so rapidly that he contemplates harvesting crops from the sea.

These changes dictate an ever stronger United Nations. In fifteen years, it has grown to become a much larger organization and in some ways a much stronger organization than the UN of 1946. It must continue to grow.

The word "stronger" must necessarily concern every phase of United Nations activity. It means more precise law to govern the relations between people of the world. It means a vast amount of machinery for adjustment of ever more difficult problems. It includes the possibility of the United Nations assuming sovereignty and administering authority in some areas such as outer space.

The United Nations has been and can be strengthened in a number of ways. The first is by a more loyal and imaginative fulfillment of their obligations by the member states. This fulfillment is the subject of the last chapter.

Other means by which the United Nations can be expanded and strengthened are:

By a more liberal interpretation of the Charter;

By the expansion of existing machinery and the addition of new bodies as the need is revealed;

By having administrative authority in those areas not under national sovereignty, such as outer space;

By greater use of the International Court of Justice and the development of world law;

By a constant approach toward universality;

By having an independent source of income;

By the revision of the text of the Charter.

The last is the ultimate way to strengthen the United Nations.

Liberal vs. Strict Constructionists

The liberal interpretation of the United Nations Charter reminds one of early American constitutional history. The strict constructionists have asserted that the United Nations could do nothing that was not spelled out in the Charter. The liberal constructionists have been willing that the United Nations assume, by agreement of an appropriate number of its members, such authority as is necessary to fulfill the purposes of the Organization as defined in the language of the Charter.

The Soviet Union has led the strict constructionist bloc as far as the political and security articles of the Charter are concerned. It has objected to the increasing use of the General Assembly at the expense of the Security Council. Practically everything undertaken by the General Assembly which seems to be at the expense of the Security Council is to the Soviet Union illegal. The USSR objected to the establishment of the Little Assembly. It objected to the Uniting for Peace Resolution and the establishment of UNEF. The Soviet Union would restore the United Nations as an organization controlled by the Security Council with full use of the veto.

Article 2 (7) is one of the articles which has been a source of debate between the strict and liberal constructionists. This article provides that "Nothing contained in the present Charter shall authorize the United Nations to intervene in matters which are essentially within the domestic jurisdiction of any state. . . ." Here the colonial powers are the strict constructionists. Most of these powers have felt that the General Assembly has gone too far in interfering in colonial matters. For illustration, they have objected to the Assembly's appointing a committee to assess reports submitted under Article 73 (e). This article provides that members shall report on various economic and social conditions in their non-self-governing areas. Nevertheless, the General Assembly has concerned itself with such matters.

Fortunately, in critical days there has usually been a large majority of the members of the United Nations who supported a liberal construction of the Charter. At any particular moment, the majority has been willing that the Organization grow and expand to meet the needs of the time. During most of the life of the United Nations, the United States has been numbered among the liberal constructionists.

The Uniting for Peace Resolution provides one of the most spectacular illustrations of a liberal interpretation of the Charter. The framers of the Charter did not contemplate the General Assembly assuming powers at the expense of the Security Council. However, few of them would now object to the assumption of such power under Articles 10, 11 and 12, which define the authority of the General Assembly in general terms. As is frequently the case in constitutional history, broad provisions of a constitution are given a precise meaning to enable a government to function.

Articles of the Charter have been used as a basis for broad statements of principle, which in time become generally accepted and tend to have a binding force upon the members. The Economic and Social Council early established the guiding principles that made possible the technical assistance program, vast in concept, if not yet in financial scope. This historic statement was made by authority of Article 66, paragraph 2 of the Charter, which provides that the Economic and Social Council "may, with the approval of the General Assembly, perform services at the request of members of the United Nations and at the request of specialized agencies."

Strength through Additional Bodies

The United Nations has been strengthened and enriched by the addition of new bodies. Some are specialized agencies dealing with economic and social problems. Other agencies have or will have a bearing on political problems. The International Atomic Energy Agency won new ground in the effort for greater United Nations authority when its Statute provided that the veto could not be used to prevent the United Nations inspectors from visiting recipient countries to verify the fact that the atomic material received was not being diverted to military purposes.

Man's exploration of outer space may prompt another agency with greater supranational authority than the International Atomic Energy Agency. In 1959, the General Assembly established a standing committee to consider what the United Nations should do about outer space activities. One year previously, the Russians themselves had suggested the establishment of a United Nations agency to prevent military experiments in outer space and to co-ordinate peacetime exploration. Unfortunately, they linked their suggestion with a demand for the elimination of strategic bases.

Consequently, the Western powers summarily dismissed the Russian suggestion.

The possibility of a disarmament organ so broad in scope as to be a new security agency of the United Nations is discussed later in this chapter.

UN Sovereignty

One of the most effective ways of giving the United Nations strength would be to give it sovereign authority in areas where no nation has extended its claims of national sovereignty. There are three such areas: Antarctica; the bed of the sea beyond the continental shelf; and outer space.

As for the first, the nations have moved to prevent Antarctica from being cut up for sovereign claims or used for military purposes. The nations that have explored in Antarctica attended a conference in Washington in 1959. They agreed to a program of co-operation for the development of this area. Both the United States and the Soviet Union have refused to recognize any territorial claims made by others in the area. It would not take too much imagination to establish the principle of United Nations sovereignty in Antarctica.

As for the bed of the sea beyond the continental shelf, there is danger that nations will try to mark off vast areas of the sea for fishing rights, to explore resources, and to find crops of food that might be harvested from the sea. From the military standpoint, the tradition of the freedom of the seas has been violated in rather a large way by several of the great powers. Recently, the President of the United States was urged to protest the Soviet government's warning that for a certain number of days nations should avoid a vast area in the Pacific where the Soviet Union was to hold missile experiments. The President replied that he could not very well make such a protest, since the United States previously had asked the nations to stay out of hundreds of thousands of square miles in the Pacific in which it was holding nuclear tests.

An expansion of United Nations sovereignty to outer space would seem to be particularly pressing. Certainly the doctrine of freedom of the seas should not be a precedent for a doctrine of freedom of the air. Many wars have been fought over freedom of the seas. The nations cannot afford even one war to assure the freedom of the outer air. One hopes that the nations will have as much imagination in extending United Nations law to outer space as they have in planning to send vehicles to celestial bodies.

The Quiet World Court

One major body of the United Nations, the International Court of Justice, has not evolved and expanded in fifteen years. In fact, a comparison would show that it has been possibly less widely used than was the Permanent Court of International Justice associated with the League of Nations. In the frantic, changing times of the last fifteen years, the nations have sought political settlements, sometimes for propaganda purposes, rather than a judicial settlement based upon law. The nations have not sufficiently committed themselves to a rule of law, nor have they given adequate attention to its development.

According to American authorities, including the President, the Vice President and the Secretary of State, the World Court has been further handicapped by the so-called Connally Reservation affixed to the United States acceptance of the compulsory jurisdiction of the Court. When the United States ratified Article 36 of the Court Statute, by which it accepted reciprocally the compulsory jurisdiction in legal disputes, it reserved to itself the right to determine what issues are domestic and therefore not subject to the

jurisdiction of the Court. Some other nations were quick
to follow the American reservation.

UN Advances toward Universality

The United Nations has been strengthened as it has moved
toward universality. Five years ago, when the author undertook a review of the first ten years of the United Nations,
he devoted considerable attention to the devices by which
some seventeen applicants had been denied admission to
the organization. Indeed, in 1955 the Secretary-General
pointed out that less than half of the European states were
members. The Soviet Union in the Security Council vetoed
the states whose membership was desired by the Western
powers. In return, the Western powers by a process of
abstentions and negative votes made it impossible to secure
a majority of seven for the admission of those states pro-
moted by the Soviet Union.

The methods used did no credit to either side. In 1946,
the United States suggested that all states that had applied
for admission up to that time be admitted en bloc. The
Soviet Union objected, taking the position that each state
should be considered individually. The following year, the
Soviet Union proposed a package admission of five applicants, after the peace treaties with Italy, Finland, Hungary,
Romania and Bulgaria had come into force. Now it was the
turn of the United States to say that each applicant should
be considered on its merits. This position was upheld by an
advisory opinion of the International Court of Justice.

The author's review of the first ten years of the United
Nations, therefore, devoted considerable attention to legal
arguments advanced by which the Soviet veto in the Security
Council could be circumvented and many new states admitted. That discussion is unnecessary five years later.

In the Tenth General Assembly, the Candian delegation

almost singlehanded succeeded over the objections of some of the great powers in breaking the log-jam on membership. Since that time, twenty-three states have been admitted, bringing the membership to eighty-two by 1960. (The unification of Syria and Egypt into the United Arab Republic reduced by one the original Charter members.)

All of the European states, with the exception of the Federal Republic of Germany and Switzerland, now belong to the United Nations. The Western powers, the Soviet bloc, and of course the new states recently freed from colonialism seem equally eager to admit any state winning its independence. Usually the colonial power is the first to sponsor the admission of its liberated colony.

There remain three divided states. Generally speaking, the smaller portions of these states are under Communist domination. The three major portions are: the Federal Republic of Germany, the Republic of Korea and Vietnam. The Soviet Union has vetoed the entrance of South Korea repeatedly. It would undoubtedly cast a veto against the admission of the other two at the present time.

But the hard core of the membership question remains. One-fourth of the population of the world—Communist China—is not represented in the United Nations by the government in effective control. Each year, a number of states move in the General Assembly for the seating of the Peiping delegates in place of the Nationalist delegates from Formosa. Each year, enough members, led by the United States, succeed without debating the merits of the case in putting the issue off to another Assembly.

Technically the problem is not one of admitting a new state. China is a Charter member of the United Nations. The question of which delegates should represent China, those from Formosa or those from the mainland, seems to be a procedural matter—which delegates' credentials should be accepted. However, the moral dilemma raised by Communist China assumes such importance that inevitably many people debate the question as if it were a matter of admitting a new state.

Without departing from the writer's view that the problem is basically a procedural one, this would be a good place to review the history of the membership provisions of the Charter.

Opposing Theories of Membership

Two opposing theories of membership were considered by the San Francisco Conference and are compromised in the Charter. One was the idea of a universal organization to which all nations would automatically belong. The other was that of an organization whose membership would be limited by good conduct.

The first United States draft of a United Nations charter, written by a committee * under the chairmanship of Under Secretary of State Sumner Welles, contained the following paragraphs:

> 1. The membership of the International Organization shall reflect the universal character of the international community.
> 2. All qualified states and dominions shall be members of the International Organization. The Council shall decide as to the nature of the qualifications.

Presumably all states that were members of the family of nations automatically were to belong to the United Nations. True, the Council was to decide upon the nature of the qualifications, but the qualifications were understood to be

* This committee of private citizens met at the State Department in 1942-43. It was composed of James T. Shotwell, Isaiah Bowman, Hamilton Fish Armstrong, Benjamin V. Cohen and Clark M. Eichelberger.

technical, such as what constitutes a state. Moral qualifications were not involved. A working paper submitted to the Welles Committee, of which the author of this book was also the author, stated:

> The United Nations might be compared to some individuals in the frontier community who have acted as vigilantes to suppress lawlessness. While they are suppressing such lawlessness they have decided to establish a reign of law and order with means of law enforcement and obligations of good behavior binding upon all nations whether they wish to consent or not.

This was the universal concept of membership. All nations were to be bound by the Charter. There could be no escape. A nation could be denied the benefits of the community because of aggression, as an individual is denied the benefits of his community if he is guilty of an offense. But the idea of admission, expulsion and withdrawal was not recognized.

Opposing the theory of universality was the belief that the United Nations should be an organization of states that have demonstrated their willingness and capacity to subscribe to certain moral standards before admission, unless, of course, they were charter members of the organization. A nation may apply; it may be admitted; it may be rejected; and it may be expelled.

The Charter represents a compromise between the two theories of membership. The spirit of the Charter and subsequent resolutions of the General Assembly anticipate universality. The obligations of the Charter, as far as the maintenance of peace is concerned, are binding upon all nations according to Article 2 (6) whether members of the Organization or not. That article provides: "The Organization shall ensure that states which are not Members of the United Nations act in accordance with these Principles so far as may be necessary for the maintenance of international peace and security."

However, the provisions of the Charter contain standards of good conduct for membership. They provide:

> 1. Membership in the United Nations is open to all other peace-loving states which accept the obligations contained in the present Charter and, in the judgment of the Organization, are able and willing to carry out these obligations.

The Dilemma of Chinese Representation

One can argue for or against seating the Peiping delegates in the United Nations depending upon which theory of membership one supports. Those opposed to seating the Peiping delegates assert that Communist China can hardly be called a peace-loving state. Thousands of American homes have memories of sons lost or imprisoned in Korea because of the intervention of Communist China in the Korean fighting. Its government is still technically at war with the United Nations in Korea. It is committing genocide in Tibet. It threatens the frontiers of India. Presumably it would add one more veto in the Security Council. Its voice in the General Assembly would be a strident one.

Those arguing for the seating of the Peiping delegates say that the United Nations should be a reflection of the world as it is. It should be a universal organization. The lawless should be brought within the law. Communist China contains one-quarter of the population of the world. Many problems of the Pacific area cannot be solved without her participation. American government officials recognize that agreements for disarmament and a cessation of nuclear tests would be meaningless without Peiping's participation. The absence of a Peiping delegate in the Security Council has had something to do with the decline of that body. It is more difficult to contemplate summit conferences in the Security Council with China represented by the delegate from Formosa.

Many members of the United Nations believe that Communist Chinese delegates should be seated in the United Nations if effective arrangements can be made for the protection of Formosa. There would be overwhelming opposition to sacrificing the Nationalists in Formosa to control from the Chinese mainland. Consequently, some members believe that there should either be two Chinas in the United Nations or that Formosa should be placed under the protection of the Organization for a period of years, so that the people on the island could exercise self-determination as to their future.

The longer the delay, the more difficult it may be to make satisfactory arrangements for Peiping's entrance. In the spring of 1950, when Trygve Lie suggested that the question of China's representation in the United Nations be dealt with, Communist China was not strong. She had just won control of the mainland. She had not committed aggression on her neighbors. She needed aid and friends. But without any help from the West, and aided principally by the Soviet Union, the Peiping regime became stronger, more aggressive and more intractable. Ten years ago, the Peiping government was very anxious to join the United Nations. Now she may be less anxious but more needed. Her bitterness has increased as she has been kept out of the family of nations and denounced, particularly by the United States. There is something quite illogical about saying that the Chinese Peoples' Republic must be bound by the obligations of the Charter but should not participate in the work of the Organization.

Degrees of Charter Revision

Talk about strengthening the United Nations by improving the efficiency of its major organs approaches the question of Charter revision. Obviously, United Nations bodies can be strengthened in some instances without revising the text of the Charter. Major changes would involve textual revision.

And as Charter review is approached, it must be recognized that there are degrees to revision. Certain changes can be made in the composition and functioning of major organs of the United Nations, while leaving the basic structure of the organization intact. The more drastic revisions which are sometimes suggested would give the Organization more supranational authority with possible legislative functions.

As for the Security Council, the use of the veto cannot be limited nor that body increased in size without a revision of the text. As for the General Assembly, much could be done to improve the efficiency of its operations through decision of its members because the Assembly is the judge of its own competence and procedure. All that would be needed would be a change in the Rules of Procedure. No Charter changes would be necessary to enhance the effectiveness of the Economic and Social Council, except to increase its size. On the other hand, to reduce the size of the Trusteeship Council, as is now necessary, or to provide for its elimination altogether when there are practically no trusteeships, would involve revision of the Charter.

The Security Council can be the most satisfactory or the most unsatisfactory body imaginable. There have been times, much rarer since 1950, when the members of the Security Council sincerely met their responsibilities. The galleries were packed; the newspapermen waited eagerly; in fact, the whole world was concentrated on the deliberations of eleven men. These were the great moments. These eleven men were aware of the responsibilities placed upon them in the Charter. One felt that the body had authority, both because of the Charter and because of the membership behind it, so its edicts could not be lightly flouted. Certainly it was easier and more comfortable for eleven men to debate and pass judgment than for eighty-two.

There have been other times when one veto has frustrated the wish of the rest of the members of the Council. There have been times when to win a point in the cold war seemed more important than reaching a decision. Then the world turned sadly away, convinced that the Security Council did not represent the hopes of the world.

If the great powers today were to put aside cold war considerations and take decisions based upon merit, the Security Council for the present and the immediate future could fulfill the responsibilities under the Charter. A summit conference could, in effect, be an emergency meeting of the Security Council which the leading statesmen could attend. Such a situation was contemplated under Article 28 (2), which provides that "the Security Council shall hold periodic meetings at which each of its members may, if it so desires, be represented by a member of the government or by some other specially designated representative." The absence of the Peiping representative from the Security Council has given the Soviet Union an excuse not to use that body for summit meetings.

It may be that the increasing size of the General Assembly and any reduction in cold war tensions will swing the pendulum back to an increasing use of the Security Council.

The Security Council

But the Security Council for the long-time pull has serious structural weaknesses. It represents a rigid power structure that will not stand the test of time. The framers of the

Charter proceeded on two false assumptions: that five powers could remain united indefinitely; that the five powers so designated would forever be the five on whose unity the success of the organization depended. The power of nations rises and falls like waves of the sea. One of the governments capable of exercising the veto in the Security Council, Nationalist China, is a government-in-exile. Who knows which will be the most powerful nations fifty years hence? Nevertheless, the Security Council is so organized that these five great powers can veto a revision of the Charter which might affect their dominance.

Other nations are going to increase in power as time goes on and they, too, will want representation on the Security Council. The League of Nations met this problem by giving ambitious states the right to re-election to the Council. Consequently, the League Council had permanent members, *de facto* permanent members and nonpermanent members. Few would wish to see this device repeated in the present Security Council.

Most of the nonpermanent seats on the Security Council are by custom earmarked geographically: two for Latin America, one for the British Commonwealth, one for Western Europe, leaving two seats to be rotated among the other members. The Soviet Union claims that one of the seats was by agreement to be earmarked for Eastern Europe. The United States denies that there was any such "gentlemen's agreement" beyond the first year of the United Nations. However, the disagreement between the two nuclear giants over this point is responsible for several deadlocked votes in the General Assembly. Sometimes the deadlock can only be broken by splitting the term. On the present Council, Poland sits for the year 1960 and Turkey will sit for the year 1961.

Latin America with its small population is quite well

represented, overrepresented in comparison with Africa. It is not realistic for a state from the Arab world periodically to be the only spokesman for Asia and Africa. Some thought must be given to representation from exploding Africa.

It has been proposed that the Charter be revised to provide for additional seats to accommodate the increasing membership of the United Nations. However, the Soviet Union has indicated that she will resist such an increase until by "gentlemen's agreement" or otherwise she is guaranteed that one of the new seats shall always be filled by a representative of Eastern Europe.

The original American working draft of the Charter provided that each geographic area should select its member or members to be elected to the Security Council. This arrangement has much to recommend it.

One device that has been suggested for the election of members to the Security Council is a plan that would be a wide modification of the method of the election of the judges to the International Court of Justice. There is no provision in the Statute that there must always be judges from the five major powers, but nevertheless there has always been a national from each of these powers on the Court. Some such method of electing the members of the Security Council would undoubtedly result in the powerful members of the world organization always being elected.

Now, quite obviously, two powers so overshadow the world that they hold the fate of mankind in their atomic stockpiles. Two others, the United Kingdom and France, have joined the atomic club. A Security Council on which these nations were not represented would ignore the power facts of life and could scarcely be responsible for the maintenance of international peace and security.

On the other hand, seventy-seven so-called small nations —and their number may soon be augmented to ninety-five

—may not be content forever to have five powers holding permanent seats in the Security Council and exercising the right of veto in the body that has the primary responsibility for the maintenance of international peace and security. Other nations are going to increase in power as time goes by and they, too, will want an equal chance to sit on the Security Council.

The ideal Security Council would be so organized as to insure that the major powers at any time would be represented without their seats being forever fixed. Obviously some special weight must be given those major powers in the Security Council who would have the major responsibility for enforcing collective security. If a United Nations Peace Force were established, this weighted influence would be less necessary.

A solution to the problem of the Security Council at present would seem to be: The powers should use the Security Council as they were supposed to use it according to the principles of the Charter. Correct the Chinese representation. Increase the size of the Security Council moderately. Face the long-range problem of drastically reforming the Security Council.

The General Assembly

A strengthening of the procedures of the General Assembly can be undertaken more quickly than a reorganization of the Security Council. The machinery of this body is capable of wide expansion without any necessary revision of the Charter. Nor is there a rigid veto with which to contend in making changes. Since all of the members of the United Nations belong to the General Assembly, they will undertake its reform with greater enthusiasm than a move to strengthen the Security Council, on which so few of them have a chance to serve.

Previous chapters have shown how the General Assembly
has assumed specific authority for peacemaking. Its moral
influence grows. It has assumed considerable legislative and
executive authority. It disposed of the colonies which Italy
surrendered at the close of the war. It partitioned Palestine.
It instructed the Secretary-General to establish a United Nations Emergency Force for the Gaza Strip and to recruit a
fleet of vessels to clear the Suez Canal.

It is inevitable that the General Assembly, growing as the
United Nations approaches universality, will be the parliament of nations. It will be the place where the hopes and
the protests of the nations can be expressed. As it approaches
universality, it will be the spokesman for over one hundred
nations in attendance. It can become a mighty moral and
legal force. It will outstrip any other body. If the past is any
indication, it will become a legislative body.

The General Assembly now has or shares a number of
bodies. The Trusteeship Council and the Economic and
Social Council report to it, and through the latter all the specialized agencies are in a sense responsible to it. The Peace
Observation Commission and the Collective Measures Committee, as well as the International Atomic Energy Agency,
are responsible to it. Undoubtedly, additional bodies will
be attached to it. It is expected that eventually there will
be an agency dealing with outer space exploration. And
many smaller states will undoubtedly insist that the proposed
disarmament agency be responsible to it as well as to the
Security Council. The General Assembly could make much
wider use of the Peace Observation Commission in the peacemaking functions which it is being forced to assume.

It has been further suggested that the General Assembly
act to give its committee structure year-round permanence.
The General Assembly is confronted by the following dilemma. If its sessions are too long, responsible statesmen

cannot attend an adequate number of meetings. If there are serious problems before it, such as Korea, it may recess instead of adjourning, as in the Seventh and Eighth Assemblies, but without leaving peacemaking machinery in its absence. It might be that various committees of the General Assembly, particularly the First (the Political and Security Committee) could either be in continuous or semicontinuous session, leaving major decisions of the plenary body to be taken in a shorter period of time.

It has been pointed out that the Fourteenth General Assembly as well as some previous Assemblies were delayed in adjourning because the Fourth Committee, dealing with trusteeship and colonial problems, had not finished its agenda. However, this Committee may have less to do as the trust agreements are liquidated and other colonial areas achieve independence.

A minor revision of the Charter might be an agreement to add to the size of the Economic and Social Council. Such expansion will not change the character of its discussions. Observers frequently point out a seeming duplication in United Nations debates. For illustration, the Second and Third Committees of the General Assembly discuss over and over again problems that have been before the Economic and Social Council. The Third Committee of the General Assembly is engaged in a long debate over clauses of the human rights covenants that have already run the gantlet of the Human Rights Commission. Not every state can be represented in the Economic and Social Council, but each state wishes to debate issues before it and takes advantage of the situation in the Second and Third Committees of the General Assembly. This duplication of debate seems inevitable until the principles of economic and social co-operation have been more fully developed and more clearly defined.

For some time the Economic and Social Council has been criticized for not giving bold leadership to the solution of world economic and social problems. This, it is said, has increased the above-mentioned Assembly debates. The decision that the thirtieth session of the Economic and Social Council in the summer of 1960 open at ministerial level is significant and timely. It will have before it the Secretary-General's proposal for a bold approach to the problem of Africa. And it may indicate a decision on the part of the major powers to give the Economic and Social Council the authority and leadership which the framers intended.

So far, this discussion has skirted a drastic revision of the Charter. If the United Nations, presumably the General Assembly, is to be given legislative powers, the right in effect to adopt binding law, a fundamental revision of the Charter is involved.

"A World of Law"

At San Francisco, the small states were unhappy with the authority given the great powers in the Security Council. As a concession to them, it was provided that the question of a Charter review conference would automatically be placed on the agenda of the Tenth Assembly if such a conference had not already been called. That Assembly could call a review conference by a simple majority.

At the Tenth Assembly, there was little sentiment among the members to hold a review conference at that time. Consequently, the Assembly, desiring to take advantage of the appropriate clause of the Charter, called a review conference in principle, but left to the Twelfth Assembly the determination of the date for such a conference. The decision has now been put off to the Sixteenth Assembly.

The fundamental problem of strengthening the United Nations by Charter revision is that the members have not

yet made up their minds how much supranational authority
they wish that organization to have. The United Nations
is in the shadowy area between a league of states and a
world government. Therein lies the dilemma of revision.

In 1948, the General Assembly authorized the Secretary-
General to ask for an advisory opinion as to whether or
not the United Nations had the authority to claim damages
from member or nonmember states for losses suffered by its
personnel in their territory. The losses had been quite tragic.
In 1949, the Court in an advisory opinion described the
nature of the United Nations in such a manner that the
late A. H. Feller, Chief Counsel to the United Nations,
compared the opinion to the famous *McCulloch* vs. *Maryland*
decision in United States constitutional history. After reviewing the obligations imposed upon the members, the
International Court of Justice decided:

> In the opinion of the Court, the Organization was in-
> tended to exercise and enjoy, and is in fact exercising
> and enjoying, functions and rights which can only be
> explained on the basis of the possession of a large meas-
> ure of international personality and the capacity to op-
> erate upon an international plane. It is at present the
> supreme type of international organization, and it
> could not carry out the intentions of its founders if it
> was devoid of international personality. It must be
> acknowledged that its Members, by entrusting certain
> functions to it, with the attendant duties and respon-
> sibilities, have clothed it with the competence required
> to enable those functions to be effectively discharged.

The Court concluded that to say the Organization has a
large measure of international personality is not the same
as saying that the United Nations is a state; still less is it the
same thing as saying it is a superstate.

Here, then, is the United Nations, an international personality, clothed by its framers with authority to operate on an international plane and whose members have taken important obligations toward it. But it is neither a state nor a world government. This dilemma is nothing to be despaired of. It is something to think through. It is inherent in the development of world society.

It has become commonplace to say that "the nations must develop a world of law." The fact that this phrase is being constantly repeated by the public and statesmen is most encouraging. It represents an important advance in thinking about the organization of the world community. How this law shall develop must be a major concern of statesmen and private citizens. The American Secretary of State was anticipating such studies when in April, 1960 he spoke of the necessity of a world of law as part of efforts at general disarmament.

Domestic law develops in various ways. One is a common acceptance of standards developing over a long period of time. This is frequently called "common law." Individuals are governed by laws established through a specific constitutional or legislative process.

International law has been developing for some three hundred years. It is still fragmentary and chaotic. It began with the acceptance by nations of certain rules of conduct toward diplomatic representatives. Later it concerned itself with the rules of so-called civilized warfare. As yet, a legislative process as we know it in the domestic community has not developed. The nearest thing to such a process in formulating international law is through the ratification of international conventions.

With the organization of the world community, first in the League of Nations and then in the United Nations, common standards of conduct were accepted by the members. The United Nations Charter imposes upon its members considerable pooling of sovereignty. This in effect means the nations are bound by law. In regard to peace and war, the obligations of the Charter are very specific. The members shall fulfill in good faith the obligations assumed by them in the Charter. All members shall settle their international disputes by peaceful means and in such a manner that peace and justice are not endangered. They shall refrain from the threat or use of force. They shall give the United Nations every assistance in any action it takes in accordance with the present Charter and shall refrain from giving assistance to an aggressor. And most significantly the Charter provides, in Chapter I, Article 2, paragraph 6, that "the Organization shall ensure that states which are not members of the United Nations act in accordance with these Principles so far as may be necessary for the maintenance of international peace and security."

The principles of the Charter are constantly being invoked in the United Nations. As recently as March 30, 1960, the United States declared in the Security Council that to promote human rights and fundamental freedoms was a positive obligation of the Charter. Resolutions of the General Assembly which are repeatedly invoked add to the body of international law.

Various bodies of the United Nations produce regulations in many fields. These tend to become accepted standards of behavior. It is agreed that the World Health Organization may proclaim international health standards which are binding on all members which do not specifically object. It is anticipated that the International Atomic Energy Agency will produce universal standards and safeguards against the hazards of nuclear development which will be accepted by all states.

As the International Court of Justice becomes more

widely used, its decisions and advisory opinions will add to the body of international law.

This acceleration of international regulations does not satisfy those who believe that there must be established in the United Nations, presumably in the General Assembly, a legislative process which could pass laws binding upon members and individuals in certain political and security matters.

The phrase "limited world government" is frequently used. It recognizes that the specialized agencies, in their varied procedures, can at best produce standards for the control of international civil aviation, atomic health safeguards, international sanitary codes, etc. There would be left to the General Assembly a limited legislative function in political and security matters where a free exercise of national sovereignty would mean disaster.

Suggestions for Weighted Voting

It is also asserted that if the General Assembly is to have such legislative powers in those limited fields it must have a system of weighted voting. If the Assembly is to be a parliament passing laws, it is argued, the vote of the greater powers should count more than the vote of the least significant members.

Many ingenious plans for weighted voting in the General Assembly have been put forward. None has been found acceptable. Certainly, weighted voting cannot be based on wealth and resources. Man would hate to establish between nations the property qualifications that he long ago discarded for the domestic franchise. Weighted voting could scarcely be based on any arbitrary standards, such as literacy. The nation with one of the highest standards of literacy in Europe has been chiefly responsible for two world wars in our generation. If based on population without a ceiling, two nations would account for nearly half of the votes in the General Assembly. These objections are not cited here to say that the problem is insoluble, but to say that it will require very considerable study. The most drastic proposal as an alternative to weighted voting in the General Assembly would be a fundamental reform of the Security Council to make it in a sense the "upper house" of a legislative body composed of the Security Council and the General Assembly.

Fresh light may be thrown on the power balance in the General Assembly and the Security Council through an approach to disarmament. For the first time, statesmen are considering what a completely disarmed world would be like. If military establishments are to disappear and nations left with nothing but local constabularies to keep internal order, the international community must provide collective security. In addition to the laws of good behavior which the nations have accepted in the Charter, additional law governing nations will be necessary. A legislative procedure for producing such law beyond the international convention method would seem to be required.

An international police force would be inevitable. Obviously, the constabulary to keep order required by the Soviet Union and the United States would be larger than the constabulary of a very small state. But a constabulary of a large state armed with sticks and stones could invade a small state. Hence, the need for the international police force. Will a separate agency for inspection and control be set up as an integral part of the United Nations? Or will the General Assembly or the Security Council, or both, be expanded to absorb these security functions? Thus as the world contemplates total disarmament, it must contemplate a very considerable addition to its peace machinery.

What of Charter review? It is the history of constitutions

that in a moment of idealism and crisis people adopt a rule of conduct which may be difficult for them to live up to when the heroic mood passes. Then they are forced to follow the rules of conduct which they would not adopt if they were to write their constitution at that time. This is the history of the UN Charter. The time for review of the Charter is in another moment of idealism and crisis, when the basic document can be revised to be stronger than the original. That time has not yet come. The nations have not yet matched the idealism of 1945. Many have been afraid of Charter review up to now for the reason that revision might result in a retreat from the obligations written into the Charter in 1945.

In 1955 the nations shied away from a review of the Charter because they lacked a challenge in the light of which the Charter could be strengthened. The movement for general and complete disarmament under international control may provide this challenge. However, revision may not be accomplished through a review conference as contemplated in Article 109 of the Charter. It is more likely that, having decided upon the strengthened security machinery necessary, the nations will then revise the Charter to meet this plan. This is different from approaching the revision of the Charter as an academic exercise.

The time for broad study by the public has arrived. In 1942 President Roosevelt asked Under Secretary Sumner Welles to initiate studies on what the new world order should be like. It might be time for another committee of private citizens to study how the law-making process of the United Nations and its security machinery should be strengthened to meet the challenge of the nuclear and outer space age. The work of such a committee should be accompanied by wide public discussion.

VII

ATTITUDE OF MEMBERS

Any review of how the United Nations has functioned in its first fifteen years must take into consideration the attitude of its members.

After fifteen years, the members have not yet made up their minds what they want the United Nations to be. They have not yet decided the extent of the contributions they wish to make to it. They have not determined how far they wish to go in developing the world organization into a growing, dynamic international society serving for nations and indeed for individuals what a government does in the domestic community—bringing people together into a civilized way of life based on law.

Use of the United Nations to deal with great political and economic problems has ebbed and flowed like the tide. There have been moments of great use and of sad neglect. Sometimes the lights have burned all night as the Security Council or the General Assembly met around the clock to prevent war. The day-to-day work goes on at New York headquarters and throughout the world. However, sometimes one looks at the bulletin board of projected meetings in the delegates' entrance and sees practically nothing scheduled.

For dramatic comparison, review how the nations dealt with major threats to world peace in 1958 as compared to

1959. In 1958, the United Nations was the source of world headlines, because the Security Council, the General Assembly and the Secretary-General in a series of complex operations dealt with the major threat to peace in that year—the Middle East. The Western Powers took the lead in insisting that this problem be dealt with in and through the United Nations.

Consider how the nations dealt with the major threat to world peace in 1959—Germany. A summit conference was projected without any relationship to the United Nations. And the foreign ministers, to prepare the way for such a meeting, conferred in Geneva, outside of the moral framework of the United Nations. In fact, the only agreement of this conference was to establish the ill-fated ten-member disarmament committee outside of the world organization.

The Secretary-General, reporting to the Fourteenth General Assembly, said: "The past year has been characterized by intense diplomatic activities mainly outside the United Nations although in some cases within its precincts or in informal contact with the Organization."

The fundamental question could be stated in another way: Is the United Nations the foundation of international policy or an instrument which nations can use or reject as short-sighted self-interest dictates?

An examination of the Charter's Preamble, purposes and principles leads to the inescapable conclusion that the framers of the United Nations contemplated a dynamic international society. The world was at war. The peoples of many nations were serving together and making terrible sacrifices to win the war. They believed that with peace would come an international society strong enough to prevent war and build a just international order. The Atlantic Charter expressed this belief.

It is only necessary to consider the objectives of the United Nations as set forth in the Preamble of the United Nations Charter to prove that the United Nations was intended to be more than an instrument of diplomatic choice. Some of these objectives bear upon the elimination of war and the establishment of collective security. Consider such phrases as: "to save succeeding generations from the scourge of war . . . to unite our strength to maintain international peace and security; to ensure, by the acceptance of principles . . . that armed force shall not be used, save in the common interest." Other objectives look toward the establishment of "conditions under which justice and respect for . . . treaties and other sources of international law can be maintained; to practice tolerance and live together in peace. . . ." Still other objectives look toward human rights and economic and social advancement: "to reaffirm faith in fundamental human rights . . . to promote social progress . . . to employ international machinery for the promotion of economic and social advancement of all peoples."

But the Charter goes further. There is the next phrase: "have resolved to combine our efforts to accomplish these aims." If the United Nations is the foundation of policy, peoples and their governments will feel an obligation to add to its strength and use it for the settlement of their problems. Under such a concept the United Nations will inevitably grow. It will increasingly become a society of peoples bound together with extensive ties of association. It will transcend the barriers of narrow nationalism.

These were the hopes and determinations of a world at war. If these hopes dim as the memory of the war recedes and the nations treat the United Nations as an instrument of policy, a diplomatic tool to be used as a matter of convenience and an organ of propaganda, the Organization will tend to become an instrument of governments, not of peoples. The foreign offices, and frequently the more timid members of such foreign offices, will determine at any moment what instrument shall be used to carry out their policies. When increasingly storms come, there will be grave danger that the United Nations will be by-passed because men of little imagination would lack the policies and the boldness necessary for success through the United Nations. These men would fall back on old ways of meeting grave world problems, even though these methods have given them the major failures of the twentieth century.

By 1960, eighty-two nations belong to the United Nations. Most of them belong because they believe in the broader concept of what the United Nations represents. These eighty-two members have different historical and cultural backgrounds and are at different levels of economic, social and political development. It is a tribute to the intensity of the United Nations spirit and the desire of most nations to contribute to the international community that the eighty-two are able to fit themselves so quickly within the principles, the machinery and the parliamentary practices of the Organization.

Different Standards and Attitudes of Members

Possibly one could consider the membership of the United Nations in five divisions:

One division would contain the four great powers, who, with Nationalist China, exercise the right of veto in the Security Council. By virtue of this veto and permanent seats in the Security Council, they are given exceptional authority, because it was felt they were in a position to make an exceptional contribution. To these four might be added Italy and Japan and a few other similar great powers. These are the nations that might labor under the delusion that they were powerful enough to go it alone without the

United Nations. They have participated in a long history
of power politics. They could argue that they do not need
the protection of the United Nations. They could say,
therefore, it is not incumbent upon them to make any special contribution to it. But in an age of nuclear warfare
and the threat from outer space weapons, it is an illusion
for them to believe that they could be secure outside the
law of the world community and without the co-operation
of the other members of the human family.

A second group would contain the old-line middle powers.
Here one thinks to a considerable extent of the nations of
Northern and Western Europe and the members of the
British Commonwealth. They are states in the main with
a traditional experience in international relations. They
have a considerable sophistication in world politics. They
represented much of the ideas and hope of the League of
Nations.

In this group, the Scandinavian countries, the Low Countries, and the members of the British Commonwealth, particularly Canada, have shown at times an exceptional single-
mindedness in their willingness to support high principles
in the United Nations with positive action. The role of
Canada has been one of the most outstanding. Her power
position is unique. Canada is a member of the British Commonwealth and shares three thousand miles of unfortified
frontier with the United States. She shares the Western
frontier without having participated in the excess of pioneer isolationism of the United States. She shares the traditions of the British Empire without participating in a
spirit of colonialism. It was the Canadian delegate who
found a formula for breaking the deadlock which was keep-
ing many states out of the United Nations. The Canadian
Minister for External Affairs, Lester B. Pearson, in the debates over Suez suggested a United Nations Emergency Force.

The suggestion was instantly supported by the representative of the United States, Ambassador Henry Cabot Lodge.

Several nations make a greater per capita contribution to
United Nations technical assistance than the United States
or any other large power. Sometimes the role of the smaller
states in the United Nations is determined by the excel-
lence of their representatives, as has been the case of the
Philippines and Ceylon.

It is the Soviet Union, of course, more than any power,
which has maintained a position of fixed rigidity in the
political phase of the United Nations and a position of ob-
structionism in its other activities. In practically all areas
there has been that hard rock, that fixed position, that un-
willingness to compromise, to negotiate; only willingness
to veto. Yugoslavia, despite her break with the USSR, votes
with her on most issues before the United Nations. Consequently, for some years there has been a solid bloc of
nine Communist states, frequently ten, which have not been
permitted to exercise choice or objectivity in their United
Nations votes.

It may not be wholly accurate to group the Latin-American states in one category. They have not always voted
together. But in the main they have stood for identical principles. They have made an important contribution in upholding the principles of justice and equity. It is to be
expected that the Latin-American members would contribute much to any strengthening of the rule of law and a
broader role for the World Court. But, unfortunately, their
idealism is too seldom matched by financial or other material contributions to such United Nations emergency efforts
as UNEF, expanded technical assistance or the problem
of refugees.

The Latin-American states are in a unique position. They
are members of the oldest and most clearly developed re-

gional organization, the Organization of American States. It has been brought closely within the framework of the United Nations. This advantageous position enables them to ask for and secure two seats in the Security Council, three seats on the Economic and Social Council and four judges on the World Court. This is, in fact, a much stronger representation in United Nations bodies than Asian states enjoy.

Beginning with 1955, the membership of the United Nations has increased rapidly. It will undoubtedly grow from eighty-two to one hundred within the next few years. One-fourth of the United Nations membership is carved out of the old colonial empires. These are the states which are the most vigorous in their protestations against colonialism. These are the states which contain the people who are the most underprivileged. Many of them represent ancient cultures which have enriched the world. Many of these peoples whose civilizations go back to antiquity have been up a blind alley economically. It may be expected that if they can develop their economies while they preserve their freedom they may experience a renaissance which will add richly to the cultural development of the future.

These states are sometimes called the Bandung Powers and sometimes the Asian-African bloc. Meeting at Bandung, Indonesia, in 1955, they surprised the West by adopting some liberal resolutions in support of the United Nations.

The Less Developed Members

One might say that of the eighty-two members of the United Nations only a minority have a substantial margin to contribute to the international community. Only a minority of the members have reached that stage of development where they have a large margin to contribute in the way of leadership, resources, money, time, manpower and technical know-how to the development of the world community over and above their own needs.

A comparison might be drawn to illustrate what is meant, by reference to the domestic community. In the simplest such community, the citizens have at least some aspect of citizen responsibility, such as respect for law, some moment at which to vote, a few pennies to pay in taxes, or some slight service over and above the basic needs of food and shelter. Without some contribution from the citizens, there could be no state. As a middle class grows, there is a greater number of the population which has more to contribute to the collective society.

So with nations. However, the newest and most under-privileged of the family of nations have something that they can contribute to the world organization. It is something of great value. It is hope, idealism and a desire for justice. These are the qualities that enable the representative of a very new state appearing in the General Assembly for the first time to speak with impassioned eloquence in the name of justice and liberty.

This situation presents the prosperous and privileged part of the world, to a great extent the Western world, with a great responsibility and opportunity. This is the responsibility of assistance to the new states on an equal and digni-fied basis. Granted that only a minority of the nations of the world today have a physical and scientific margin to contribute to the development of the international com-munity. And granted that too few nations today must carry the burden of world financing and world political security. Still, what an opportunity there is for the few to help the new nations, representing overwhelmingly the population of the world, to that condition of prosperity and stability where they too have a substantial margin to contribute to an international society.

It cannot be done successfully on a bilateral basis. It cannot be done by asking these nations to choose one side or the other in the game of power politics. It can only be done through the United Nations, which to them represents the ideals of equality and freedom.

It would be to the advantage of all states that the relative dominance of four or five powers be reduced. It would be better for all states that there be many nations of the world who can assume their share of responsibility for the maintenance of peace and the development of the community of nations.

Some of the newest and smallest states while receiving help develop a considerable margin to contribute to helping others. Israel, for illustration, is one of the larger exporters of technical assistance. She has organized the Black Star Steamship Line with Ghana and her technical assistance experts roam as far as Thailand. In any rational order of the Middle East, she would be able to supply much of the technical know-how for its economic development.

India, despite her neutralist reaction to the power politics of the atomic giants, at present is the largest contributor of troops to UNEF in the Middle East.

Ironically, some of the new states, recently freed from colonialism and extremely critical of the older powers, are very sensitive to criticisms of mistakes which they themselves might be making. India might be said to lead the anticolonial bloc in the United Nations. However, she must bear a considerable responsibility for failure to hold the United Nations plebiscite in Kashmir, which she promised to support. Indonesia, in her effort to liquidate the rest of the Dutch Empire in the Pacific, would become an empire herself by annexing Western New Guinea, for which she has very little justifiable claim.

Many of the Asian and African states seem to have a double standard in their attitude toward Western oppression and Communist oppression. Some of the states that properly protested South Africa's apartheid policies abstained in the votes condemning Soviet conduct in Hungary and Communist Chinese violation of human rights in Tibet.

The great powers, the middle powers and the Latin-American bloc place a considerable emphasis on the maintenance of international peace and the development of the principles of collective security. The Communist states emphasize such principles in terms of Soviet ideology.

In comparison, the Asian and African states say much less about political settlements than they do about economic development, and violation of human rights, as in South Africa. The United Nations is a household word in some Asian-African states because of the work of UNICEF or the specialized agencies.

The Hesitant Great Powers

It has been said that each nation is half in and half out of the United Nations to the extent that at times it contributes much and gains much from the organization and at other times forgets or fails to use it. This is particularly true of the great powers. Frequently, in neglecting to use it, a nation is failing to tap the United Nations' mine of potential power.

France presents a tragic example of such failure. Several nations wanted to bring the Indo-Chinese question to the United Nations. Had this been done, as the problem of Indonesia was brought to it a few years previously, the tragedy of Dienbienphu might have been avoided and the

Geneva Conference of 1955, disastrous as far as France was concerned, might never have been held. Her policy of wanting to go it alone was a serious mistake from the standpoint of national interest.

Between the First and Second World Wars, France was one of the strongest advocates of collective security at the League of Nations. She was one of the most fertile minds in the League of Nations. A statesman remarked one time at Geneva that when a problem was before the League of Nations there would always be two plans, the draft submitted by the Secretariat and the draft of the French. But following the Second World War, French policy has been less concerned with the over-all world community than with the development of the European community. Smarting under the memory of a humiliating occupation, anxious for the restoration of French prestige, and resentful over United Nations debates on Algeria, the French President's eloquence on world matters seems limited exclusively to technical assistance for underdeveloped areas.

As for Great Britain, she seems to have exhibited the same unevenness of support as the government of the United States—at times important contributions, and at other times neglect. Certainly, the votes in the General Assembly and the Security Council would indicate Britain votes usually on the side of constructive action. As expected, Britain supported intervention in Korea and was the second largest contributor of forces to the United Nations army resisting aggression.

British public opinion, first in support of the League of Nations and then of the United Nations, has been clearly expressed. A large section of British people supported the United Nations against their own government in Suez in 1956. One wonders in how many countries the United Nations Association would have had the courage, and in fact the liberty of choice, which the British Association expressed in support of the United Nations against its own government in Suez.

The Soviet government continues to believe in a dictatorship of the four great policemen in the United Nations. That government's use of the veto in the Security Council indicates that the Soviet intended this dictatorship to function according to its wishes.

Russia

Having failed to maintain a dominant position in the Security Council by the veto and feeling itself overwhelmingly outvoted in the General Assembly, the Soviet Union has turned to the device of parity. This device, which it wishes to carry out in the United Nations or outside the United Nations, is a strange concept. It is best illustrated by the ten-nation disarmament committee, which was set up outside the United Nations. This committee was composed of five Western powers—the United States, the United Kingdom, France, Italy and Canada—and also five Communist states—the Soviet Union, Poland, Romania, Czechoslovakia and Bulgaria. Inherently, there would seem to be no parity in this arrangement. One can scarcely equate the military and industrial importance of Romania and Poland, to say the least, with the strength of Italy and Canada. However, the arrangement has an all-important aspect of parity from the Communist point of view. The Eastern states are Communist states which will vote as a bloc with the Soviet Union. The Western states are democracies which will tend to vote similarly, although not under the dictatorship of any one of them.

Sometimes the Soviet Union's idea of parity is for a committee to be composed of a certain number of Communist states and a balanced number of Western powers, to which are added a number of neutrals. These neutrals, though they may not be able to make an important contribution to the issue at hand, would tend to follow a policy of neutrality, at least to the extent of not voting automatically for or against either side. In 1958, the Soviet Union objected to the composition of the United Nations outer space committee and refused to join it. Consequently, two of the neutral members, United Arab Republic and India, refused to accept their membership on that committee lest they be too closely identified with the Western position. In 1959, when more neutrals and Communist states were added, the Soviet Union assumed its place on the expanded committee.

The blame for much of the frustration in the United Nations rests with the Soviet Union, which cannot tolerate being outvoted in the democratic processes. However, it must be pointed out that frequently the Western states, and particularly the United States, have forced a vote in the General Assembly when such a vote was not vital to the preservation of peace. The desire seemed to be to register overwhelming majorities against the Soviet Union. The United States, as have other great powers, has used United Nations bodies, including the General Assembly, as places to wage the cold war. If the author seems to devote more attention to the contribution and neglect of the United States, it is because the book is written from the American point of view. The policy of the United States toward the United Nations has vibrated between the highest idealism and calculated neglect. It is a record of contrast and improvisation.

Positive Role of the United States

On the plus side, the United States has been in a position to do more for the United Nations than any other great power, and it has done so. The American people were happy to have had a few acres in the heart of their most populous city contributed as international territory for the capital of the United Nations. In United Nations emergency projects, such as for Arab refugees and UNEF, the financial contribution of the United States has been most generous.

At the time when the United States was the sole possessor of the atomic bomb it offered to scrap its atomic program and therefore its considerable military advantage in return for adequate inspection and control. It made most advanced suggestions for a supranational United Nations authority in a specific area when it suggested that an international commission be empowered to punish the nation or the individual violating atomic agreements. And this without the right of great power veto!

It was the United States that challenged the United Nations to meet aggression at the Thirty-eighth Parallel in Korea. This country contributed overwhelmingly the greatest number of troops and suffered thousands of casualties in support of this effort.

At times, the United States has contributed much toward the evolution of the United Nations. It suggested the Uniting for Peace Resolution, which shifted the center of gravity from the Security Council to the General Assembly. It was the first to suggest that the Collective Measures Committee make a study of a United Nations Legion. The Point Four Program of President Truman inspired the Expanded Technical Assistance Program. The United States government has had much to do with the Declaration of Human Rights. No more dramatic challenge has ever been made to the United Nations than that contained in President Eisenhower's Atoms for Peace speech.

Negative Role of the United States

One could begin the minus side of the ledger by referring to what happened to delay implementing the suggestions in President Eisenhower's Atoms for Peace speech. The President suggested an atoms for peace agency. A small com-

mittee met in Washington outside the United Nations
to draft a statute. The General Assembly showed its ma-
turity in insisting on the right of debate and made so many
suggestions for the revision of the statute that the United
States government enlarged the committee and rewrote the
preamble. It was then submitted to the delegates of eighty-
two nations who met at the United Nations headquarters.
Finally, the International Atomic Energy Agency was established with a more intimate relationship to the United
Nations than that of the specialized agencies.

The Agency was to have several main purposes. It was to
act as a bank of fissionable material for the nations that
needed such material. The principle of inspection without
the veto was accepted. United Nations inspectors could assure themselves that the material contributed would not
be diverted for military purposes. Of equal importance was
the purpose of the Agency to establish uniform safeguard
and health standards.

The prospect of the application of atomic energy to peaceful uses was hailed as the beginning of the second industrial revolution. It was said that the Agency would enable
mankind to use atomic energy while avoiding the unfortunate social and human consequences of the first industrial
revolution.

And how have the nations lived up to this dream? How
have they used the Agency?

The United States government has made over forty bilateral arrangements outside the Agency. The British have
made ten and the Russians fifteen. It is true that many of
these arrangements were made before the Agency was completed. However, the government of the United States at
least gave the impression that if the General Assembly accepted the principle of inspection without the veto, the
United States would bring its bilateral agreements under

the Agency. With three exceptions, none of the American bilateral arrangements has been tied in. In only one instance, the agreement with Japan, has the Agency functioned as a bank of fissionable material—material which the Canadian government contributed without cost to the Agency.

There are reasons why the Agency has not functioned as originally planned as a bank of fissionable material. It was anticipated after the war that there would be a deficit in conventional power and that atomic energy would be needed quickly. Instead, there is a surplus of conventional power among the highly industrialized nations and atomic energy for power purposes has not yet become an important need of the underdeveloped areas. However, the latter situation may be but temporary.

But there is a crying need for universal health standards and safeguards. The Atomic Energy Agency was charged with the development of rules and standards, in fact, world law, in an area of great need, in an area fraught with danger for the future. The great powers, particularly the United States, have prevented the Agency from performing this task.

The attitude of the United States toward the United Nations has been like that of all other states, half in and half out. Bold as our policy has been at times, as in Korea, we have not consistently used the full resources and capacities of the Organization to build a world of peace and security. Support has fluctuated. Sometimes the United States apparently forgets to use the United Nations, as at the time when it proposed a plan for the containment of Communism by means of military aid to Greece and Turkey without informing the American representative at the United Nations in advance of this drastic step. Too frequently Americans expect the United Nations to do exactly what they want. At times the U.S.A. has failed to use the United Nations for conciliation, but has rather used it as an instrument of propaganda in the cold war. And as a people Americans tend to become disillusioned and impatient.

American policy in the United Nations sometimes gives the impression of improvisation with the lack of a carefully thought-out policy to reap the fruits of a good position. In 1956, the United States was the only great power with membership on the Security Council willing to oppose use of armed force in violation of the Charter from whatever source. It was willing that the Charter be invoked against the British, French and Israelis in Suez and the Soviet Union in Hungary.

Never has the prestige of the United States in the United Nations been higher. One would have expected that the United States government would have followed its advantage in the General Assembly by demanding constructive solutions of outstanding problems, particularly in the Middle East. Indeed, the American representative introduced a draft resolution looking toward some constructive solutions. In the face of opposition, the draft was not pressed. But it would seem that the United States was in a sufficiently good position to insist, to insist and insist again on progressive measures. Such insistence would have given the United States the offensive in the Assembly in demanding a fresh approach to some issues that had dragged on altogether too long.

Instead, to the consternation of almost everyone and the dismay of the smaller states, the play was suddenly taken away from the American delegation in the General Assembly and the game was played out in Washington. Suddenly, the Secretary of State announced the "Eisenhower Doctrine." Congress was asked to give the President authority to employ the armed forces of the United States to secure and protect the territorial and political independence of any nation in the Middle East requesting such aid against overt armed aggression by international Communism.

The author of this book appeared before the Senate and House Foreign Relations Committees to urge that nothing be done to by-pass the United Nations or to weaken the American position in the Organization at the moment when American prestige was at the very highest.

The various warnings were not followed. The "Eisenhower Doctrine" was announced; it was given the most cursory relationship to the United Nations. And so at the moment of victory in upholding the principles of the Charter in the Middle East, the United States by-passed the United Nations to announce a unilateral security role in the Middle East.

Some of the choices confronting the United States in regard to use of the United Nations are difficult ones. But the answers are obvious. Aid to underdeveloped areas presents an illustration of a difficult choice. This problem is further spelled out in Chapter IV, "Standards in Larger Freedom." The United States government is challenging its NATO partners to make greater contributions to the underdeveloped areas. The choice is: to encourage these nations to join with this country in an open competition with the Soviet Union in giving such aid or to channel it through the United Nations with the Soviet Union asked to participate. The latter would seem to be the obvious choice of this government, but apparently a decision has not yet been made.

Outdated Summit Conferences

The choice of using the United Nations or by-passing it again presented itself in the attempt to hold a summit conference to meet in May, 1960.

The critics of this conference did not object to meetings

of a few at a high level. Several times the members of the General Assembly have by an overwhelming vote asked the great powers to reduce tensions between them so that the United Nations could get on with the job of peacemaking. In fact, Article 28 of the Charter provides for periodic high-level meetings under the Security Council.

After months of preparation and anticipation, four statesmen went to the summit on May 16, 1960. Their effort met with disaster. The summit conference really never got under way. A series of unexpected events made the holding of the conference very difficult. Mr. Khrushchev finally ended it by a series of impossible demands upon the President of the United States. Possibly not since the Berlin blockade have relations between the East and the West been so strained as on that fateful day in Paris.

It is doubtful that the heads of the four states will again journey to the summit as they did in May, 1960. The world may well have outgrown a meeting of the kind undertaken at Paris. For many centuries, princes, warriors and statesmen have journeyed to summit conferences to remake the map of the world, usually of Europe, after a war. They were bound by no laws nor moral principles of a community of nations. They were motivated by force, necessity and princely pride. Those days have passed. There is now an orderly society whose law is binding upon the vast majority of nations.

Mr. Khrushchev lost no time in demanding a meeting of the Security Council to receive Soviet complaints on the U-2 incident. The Soviet delegate, Mr. Gromyko, asked the Security Council to condemn American espionage over the Soviet Union. Obviously, Mr. Gromyko could hardly have expected that his resolution would secure the necessary majority of seven votes of the Security Council. It failed to be adopted.

In the meantime, on May 23, 1960, four members of the Security Council not immediately involved—Argentina, Ceylon, Ecuador and Tunisia—introduced a resolution of a different kind. They recommended to the four great powers concerned that they seek a solution of international problems by negotiation or other peaceful means as provided in the Charter of the United Nations. They requested them to continue their efforts toward disarmament and the prohibition of nuclear weapons tests under an international control system. They requested the four powers to continue their negotiations on the technical aspects of measures against the possibility of surprise attack. And they urged the four governments to resume discussions as soon as possible and to avail themselves of the assistance that the Security Council and other appropriate United Nations organs may be able to render to this end.

The representatives of the four states introducing the resolution showed wisdom both in what they asked the resolution to accomplish and in the remarks they made. Clearly these representatives did not sympathize with the Soviet Union in asking condemnation of the United States because of the U-2 incident. Neither did they hold the United States blameless. What they wanted was to re-establish negotiations on disarmament, cessation of weapons tests and reduction of tensions. These four delegates illustrate the fact that statesmen of the smaller powers having the larger interest of the world at heart may speak with a moral authority which the great powers cannot ignore. This larger interest is shown in the following quotation from the delegate of Ecuador:

> When after several years of grievous cold war, relationships between the great Powers took a conciliatory turn, a sensation of relief prevailed in the international scene and direct contacts between the Heads of Govern-

ment were universally applauded. However, two serious dangers have been perceived by those of us who have observed events from the angle of the international community in general: Firstly, the danger that the exclusive handling of problems by the great Powers might overlook the interest of all other countries; and secondly, the danger that such contacts, since they are functioning somewhat outside an established international structure, might be too greatly conditioned upon the ups and downs of the relationships between the great Powers, and that therefore they would be subject to the vicissitudes and fragility of said relationships.

Perhaps a further positive aspect of recent events is the undeniable lesson to the effect that the interests of the great Powers, as well as the interests of all other countries, would be better protected in the long run if the relationships between them and negotiations between them were clearly framed within some international law—and the greatest and highest international law is the Charter of the United Nations. If the negotiations and dealings among them with regard to the problems of universal interest were channeled through a structure which would give them stability in critical moments—which will always occur—it would be better if their dealings were conducted in the presence of the representatives of the other members of the international community whose interests are at stake and whose positive contribution cannot and must not be underestimated.

The resolution of the four passed with nine in favor and two abstentions, those of the Soviet Union and Poland. Again, the calm and sober judgment of the third force came into play. And by the third force, one means those members of the United Nations who wish to avoid involvement between the nuclear giants and hope that they may be a force powerful and wise enough to bring the giants together. Or, mixing figures of speech, the third force may form a bridge between the two.

The Secretary-General in his press statement following the breakup of the summit conference pointed out that the "Organization provides the framework for public diplomacy and for conference diplomacy on any level which Governments may desire." There are times when private conferences of a few may be required. The United Nations provides the means for such conferences. However, when a few statesmen meet under the United Nations, they are presumably influenced by its laws and its principles. There is the symbolical presence of the other members of the United Nations who are equally concerned with the decisions which, under modern conditions, affect all mankind. Furthermore, there are available the mediation talents of the Secretary-General and his able staff.

What if the summit conference had erupted in disaster and there had been no United Nations to fall back on? The situation would be desperate indeed. The world experienced relief that discussions could go on through the facilities of the Security Council and the General Assembly and with the Secretary-General and his staff.

One of the reasons for such a feeling of relief is that conferences in the United Nations are a continuous process. If a session of the Security Council or the General Assembly fails to reach a conclusion today, these bodies may meet again tomorrow. Discussions continue in some form or other. The process of conferences at the United Nations is an endless one. General Carlos P. Romulo has well suggested as an alternative to the ill-fated Paris effort that the United Nations be considered "the permanent summit."

As for the United States in its approach to the problems which the summit conference failed to discuss, it should accept the fact that the great problems of today and tomorrow can only be met successfully, with peace preserved and man's dignity and freedom guaranteed, in a universal effort in the United Nations.

Tasks for Planet Earth

The text for the conclusion of this chapter might be a sentence taken from the report to the Fourteenth General Assembly of the United Nations Committee on Outer Space. This report said: "Space activities must to a large extent be an effort of the Planet Earth as a whole."

Speaking at a meeting at the American Rocket Society in 1959, the author of this book said,

> Outer space is simply a more dramatic projection of many problems confronting mankind which must be solved by . . . Planet Earth as a whole and Planet Earth must be a moral and legal entity. Since the benefits from the use of outer space as well as the dangers will be felt by all nations and since the effort to achieve those benefits involves roaming in a vast area of outer space, it seems incredible that the efforts should be undertaken by isolated earth sovereignties.

> Another reason for establishing United Nations law in outer space and controlling all experiments is a moral one. Scientists have already pointed out the dangers of contamination; there are other moral considerations. It would reduce our generation to a final absurdity if an effort were made to plant a Soviet or an American flag on the moon and claim the right of annexation. Has man the right to attempt to make a landing on celestial bodies which may or may not be inhabited by intelligent beings? On the other hand, if man has the capacity to reach the celestial regions, should he remain in enforced isolation? Should he not attempt to make the landings? But how should he do it and with what authority and in what spirit and with what purpose are

moral considerations. What moral responsibilities or inhibitions, and what moral rights man has to invade the celestial bodies, should be matters of high moral consideration. The decision should not be taken by the citizens of any one country operating outside of universal law.

Quite obviously, the projection of United Nations law into outer space, with authority to regulate, would be an act of world government. I do not fear the term. Traditionalists in the field of international law may say that this is not the way that international law develops and will challenge the right of the United Nations to establish such institutions of government. But I say that we must have as much imagination in developing the laws and the controls for outer space as we have imagination to plan space platforms and visits to celestial bodies.

Outer space is simply a more dramatic projection of the moral, legal and technical problems confronting mankind which must be solved by an effort of Planet Earth as a whole. And Planet Earth must be a moral and legal entity.